看电影学汉语

《长江七号》视听说教程

尹冠儒　王文英　编著

河北大学出版社
·保定·

出 版 人：朱文富
责任编辑：杨 洋
装帧设计：张彦琪
责任校对：李 易
责任印制：常 凯

图书在版编目（CIP）数据

看电影学汉语.《长江七号》视听说教程 / 尹冠儒，王文英编著. -- 保定：河北大学出版社，2022.12
ISBN 978-7-5666-2136-8

Ⅰ.①看… Ⅱ.①尹… ②王… Ⅲ.①汉语－对外汉语教学－教材 Ⅳ.① H195.4

中国国家版本馆 CIP 数据核字 (2023) 第 010640 号

出版发行：河北大学出版社
地址：河北省保定市七一东路 2666 号 邮编：071000
电话：0312-5073033 0312-5073029
邮箱：hbdxcbs818@163.com 网址：www.hbdxcbs.com
经 销：全国新华书店
印 刷：保定市正大印刷有限公司
幅面尺寸：185 mm × 260 mm
印 张：9
字 数：170 千字
版 次：2022 年 12 月第 1 版
印 次：2022 年 12 月第 1 次印刷
书 号：ISBN 978-7-5666-2136-8
定 价：58.00 元

前　言
Preface

电影艺术被称为第七艺术，具有独特的艺术性和表现性，是当代社会生活中不可或缺的一部分。同时，电影包含自然的语料、真实的场景与丰富的文化内涵，是国际中文教育的良好工具，在调动学习者各种感官、引发学习者兴趣等方面有着难以比拟的优势，也有利于教师丰富教学手段、改善教学效果、活跃课堂氛围。

中文电影《长江七号》的主题积极向上，剧情精彩有趣，台词生活化且难度适中。本教材以此部电影为载体，将语言材料置于活泼生动的语境中，唤起学习者分析、模仿和运用语言的积极性，使其在欣赏过程中自然习得汉语。此外，当代中文影视作品作为中国文化的传播媒介，展现了中国社会的发展和变迁、中国人思维方式和生活方式的变化，学习者在通过中文电影提升语言技能和交际实践能力的同时，也将增进对中国社会及文化的认识。

本书定位于初级汉语学习者，基于汉语作为第二语言教学的理论与实践，如中国语言学之父赵元任的对外汉语教学思想，同时吸收第二语言习得领域的相关研究成果，如美国语言教育家斯蒂芬·克拉申（Stephen D. Krashen）的“可理解性输入假说”（The Comprehensible Input Hypothesis）和“最优输入假说”（The Optimal Input Hypothesis）等，借鉴国内外优秀外语教材的长处，以培养学习者的综合语言运用能力为宗旨。本书的特色有以下几点：突出趣味因素和沉浸式输入，激发学习者学习的主动性；注重“先语后文”的原则，融入功能和任务型语言教学的策略；参照新汉语水平考试（HSK/HSKK）的内容及题型，兼顾应试与交际，考教结合。

本书主要适用于已掌握300个以上汉语基础词汇、基本达到《国际中文教育中文水平等级标准》（GF0025—2021）中“初等一级”水平的学习者，使其在观看电影的视听基础上理解具体语料中的主要内容，运用相关句式进行准确得体的对话和成段表达，全方位提升学习者听解汉语和口语表达的能力，同时巩固和提高其基本语法知识，加强学习者读、写等方面的语言能力。

全书共23课，生词约400个，语法点62个（以《国际中文教育中文水平等级标准》中“初等”各级别的相关内容为主），建议每课的授课时间为2至3学时（45分钟/学时）。每课均设置生词、语法点及综合练习三大板块，章节后设有文化知识内容。生词来源于电影台词，标注拼音、词性及英译；语法点也选自电影对白，力求“精讲”和易懂，例句中包含该语法点在电影中的原句；综合练习包括选词填空并朗读、听后重复句子、判断句子对错、连词成句、看图造句、回答问题、角色配音及中文脱口秀八种类型。选词填空并朗读针对生词进行练习；听后重复句子参照HSKK初级、中级试题中的题型设置，录音语速适中；判断句子对错考察学习者对电影中对话的理解情况；连词成句和看图造句分别参照HSK三级和四级试题中书写部分的题型设置，针对语法点、生词进行练习；回答问题、角色配音及中文脱口秀主要训练学习者的口语表达能力。此外，书后附有听力文本和词汇总表，另可通过扫描各课听力练习中的二维码获得相关资源。

本书系河北省高等教育教学改革研究与实践项目“可理解输入视域下新型汉语国际教育视听说教材研发”（编号：2020GJJG018）、教育部中外语言交流合作中心2021年国际中文教育创新项目“一带一路沿线国家中文国际教育推广与实践——以毛里塔尼亚、老挝、印度尼西亚为例”（编号：21YH007CX3）成果。欢迎使用本书的师生反馈宝贵意见与建议，以便不断改进和完善，使之更好地为国际中文教育事业服务。

编者

2022年12月

电影简介

Movie Introduction

中文名：《长江七号》

外文名： CJ7

上映时间： 2008 年

片长： 87 分钟

导演： 周星驰

类型： 喜剧/科幻/剧情

总票房： 2.03 亿人民币

色彩： 彩色

IMDb 编码： tt0940709

获奖情况： 第 28 届香港电影金像奖最佳新演员 徐娇（周小狄扮演者）

主要人物

Movie Roles

七仔：又叫长江七号，来自外太空的生物

周铁（周爸爸）：周星驰饰，民工

周小狄：徐娇饰，周铁的儿子，博思学校小学生

陈俊生（蛋挞头）：黄蕾饰，周小狄的同学

小芬：胡倩琳饰，周小狄的同学

美娇：韩永华饰，周小狄的同学

暴龙：姚文雪饰，周小狄的同学

袁老师：张雨绮饰，博思学校老师

曹主任：李尚正饰，博思学校老师

体育老师：冯勉恒饰，博思学校老师

管工（老板）：林子聪饰，周铁的同乡

目　录

Contents

第一课　去学校 Go to School

(电影片段 00：00—03：10)

生词 Words/Phrases

1. 这么/那么	zhème/nàme	pron.	so，such
2. 脏	zāng	adj.	dirty
3. 刚才	gāngcái	n.	just now
4. 老	lǎo	adv. /adj.	always; old
5. 借口	jièkǒu	n.	excuse
6. 干净	gānjìng	adj.	clean
7. 主任	zhǔrèn	n.	director
8. 跟	gēn	prep. /v. /conj.	with; to follow; and
9. 弄	nòng	v.	to make，to do
10. 啊	a	part.	used at the end of a sentence to indicate confirmation or defense
11. 摔跤	shuāi jiāo	v.	fall down
12. 小心	xiǎoxīn	adj.	careful
13. 去世	qùshì	v.	pass away
14. 民工	míngōng	n.	farmer-laborer
15. 见面	jiàn miàn	v.	to meet
16. 把	bǎ	prep. /m.	function words; used for things with a handle
17. 拿	ná	v.	to take，to fetch
18. 擦	cā	v.	to wipe

语法点 Grammar Notes

1 趋向补语

“动词＋来/去”表示动作的方向，“来”表示朝着说话人的方向，“去”表示背离说话人的方向。常用动词有“上”“下”“进”“出”“回”“过”“起”等。简单趋向补语也可以做其他动词的补语，表示动作的方向，构成复合趋向补语，对动作进行具体的描述。宾语是处所时，要放在“来/去”之前。

“v.＋来/去” indicates the direction of an action, with “来” indicating the direction towards the speaker and “去” indicating the direction away from the speaker. The most frequently used verbs include “上”“下”“进”“出”“回”“过”“起”. Simple complement of direction can be used after another verb as its complement, that is a compound complement of direction that indicates the direction of the action and describes the action in detail. When the object is a place, it should be put before “来/去”.

例如 Example

（1）我在楼上，你**上来**吧。

（2）他**回**家**去**了。

（3）他从书包里**拿出来**一本书。

（4）不要**走过来**。（电影原句）

2 “刚才”和“刚（刚）”

“刚才”是名词，“刚（刚）”是副词，都表示动作发生的时间不长，但是“刚才”常常表示几分钟以前，而“刚（刚）”表示的短时间是对说话人来说的，可以是几分钟、几天甚至几个月。“刚才”可以用在动词前或者句子前，“刚（刚）”只能用在动词前。

The noun “刚才” and the adverb “刚（刚）” both indicate that the action has happened not long ago. However, “刚才” usually means several minutes ago, while “刚（刚）” means a short time from the speaker's point of view, which can be several minutes, a few days, even months. “刚才” can be used before the verb or at the beginning of the sentence, while “刚（刚）” is only used before the verb.

例如 Example

（1）他**刚才**喝了一杯茶。/**刚才**他喝了一杯茶。

（2）他**刚（刚）**喝了一杯茶。

（3）我**刚（刚）**来中国一个月。

（4）**刚才**上学的时候，不小心摔了一跤。（电影原句）

3 状态补语

状态补语是对动作的结果、程度、状态等进行描述或评价，常用结构助词“得”来连接动词后的状态补语。如果有宾语，要把宾语提前或重复动词；表示否定时，要把否定词放在“得”后边，口语表达中有时“得”可以省略。状态补语的疑问形式是在“得”后使用“形容词＋不＋形容词”，形成正反疑问句。

A complement of state describes or evaluates the result, degree or state of an action. The structural particle“得”is often used to introduce the state after a verb. If the verb takes an object, the object should be put before the verb, or the verb be reduplicated. In the negative form, the negative word should be put after“得”, and“得”can be omitted in oral communication. In the interrogative form,“得”is followed by the structure“adj. ＋不＋adj.”, forming an affirmative-negative sentence.

例如 Example

（1）他起**得**早。

（2）她（说）汉语说**得**很好。

（3）我睡（**得**）不好。

（4）你住**得**远不远？

（5）你怎么弄**得**这么脏啊？（电影原句）

4 “把”字句

“把”字句用来表示对确定的人或事物做出相应处置，结构为“A 把 B＋动词＋……”，多用于对别人的请求、命令。A 为动作的发出者，B 为动词涉及的对象，两者必须是特指或已知的。否定副词和能愿动词等应放在“把”字前。

A“把” sentence can be used to indicate a certain action done on a definite person or thing, the structure being“A 把 B＋v. ＋...”, is often used to request or order other people to do something. A is the agent of the action, and B is the patient, both A and B should be specific or known to the speaker and the listener. If there is a negative adverb or a modal verb etc., it should precede“把”.

例如 Example

（1）请你**把**水喝了。

（2）他没**把**书给我。

（3）妹妹**把**衣服弄得很脏。

（4）**把**它拿着。（电影原句）

综合练习 Comprehensive Exercises

一、选择恰当的词语填空并朗读 Choose the Proper Words to Fill in the Blanks and Read the Sentences Aloud

跟　干净　借口　拿　弄

❶ 请把这些杯子洗________。

❷ 你能把书________给我吗？

❸ 你不应该这么做，不要找________了。

❹ 我经常________爸爸妈妈聊天。

❺ 他把手________得很脏。

二、听后重复句子 Repeat after Listening

三、判断对错 Ture or False

❶ 周小狄一个人来学校。　（　）

❷ 曹主任很喜欢周小狄。　（　）

❸ 周小狄的妈妈去世了。　（　）

❹ 周小狄的爸爸工作不忙。　（　）

四、连词成句 Rearrange the Words or Phrases to Make Sentences

❶ 这个　这么　贵　为什么　手机 →

❷ 一杯　喝了　他　茶　刚才 →

❸ 我　把　给　请　书 →

❹ 走　他　很快　得 →

五、看图造句 Make Sentences According to the Pictures

上去　　　　回去　　　　过来

______　　______　　______

六、回答问题 Answer the Questions

❶ 周小狄为什么一个人去学校?

❷ 袁老师对周小狄怎么样?

七、角色配音 Role Play

三人一组，分别扮演周小狄、曹主任和袁老师。

八、中文脱口秀 Chinese Talk Show（1.5 分钟）

你的父母是做什么工作的?

提示：教师、律师、医生、警察、经理、店员、工人、商人、军人等。

文化知识 Cultural Knowledge

中国的教育制度

China's Education System

中国的教育一般可以分为学前教育、初等教育、中等教育、高等教育 4 个阶段。学前教育指 3 至 6 岁的儿童在幼儿园接受的教育，初等教育指 6 至 12 岁的儿童在小学接受的教育，中等教育指 12 至 17 岁的青少年在中等学校接受的教育，普通中学分为初级中学（初中）和高级中学（高中），学制各为 3 年。目前中国实行九年义务教育制度，即小学六年和初中三年。高等教育指在中等教育后进行的专科、本科和研究生教育。

China's education can be generally divided into preschool education, primary education, secondary education and higher education. Preschool education refers to the education that children receive in kindergarten during 3-6 years old. Primary education refers to the education that children aged 6-12 years receive in primary school. Secondary education refers to the education that adolescents aged 12-17 years old receive in secondary school. Ordinary secondary school is divided into junior high school and senior high school, with the length of schooling being three years each. At present, China implements nine-year compulsory education system, namely six years in primary school and three years in junior high school. Higher education refers to college education, undergraduate education and postgraduate education after secondary education.

第二课　我的志愿 My Aspiration

（电影片段 03：11—04：53）

生词 Words/Phrases

1. 志愿	zhìyuàn	n./v.	aspiration; volunteer
2. 当	dāng	v./prep.	to become; when
3. 明星	míngxīng	n.	star, celebrity
4. 片酬	piànchóu	n.	remuneration for a movie actor/actress
5. 企业家	qǐyèjiā	n.	enterpriser, entrepreneur
6. 方面	fāngmiàn	n.	aspect
7. 被	bèi	prep.	used to indicate the passive voice
8. 穷	qióng	adj.	poor, impoverished
9. 骨气	gǔqì	n.	moral integrity, strength of character
10. 吹牛	chuī niú	v.	to boast, to brag
11. 打架	dǎ jià	v.	to fight, come to blows
12. 努力	nǔlì	adj.	hard-working
13. 就算	jiùsuàn	conj.	even if
14. 受到	shòudào	v.	to receive
15. 尊敬	zūnjìng	v./n.	to respect, to esteem; respect
16. 碰	pèng	v.	to touch; to meet
17. 放	fàng	v.	to put, to place; to release

语法点 Grammar Notes

1 “被”字句

“被”字句可表达被动意义，结构为“主语＋被/叫/让＋宾语＋动词＋……”。主语一般是动作的接受者，宾语一般是动作的发出者。“被”后边的宾语可以省略，“叫”“让”后边必须有宾语。否定副词和能愿动词等应放在“被”前边。

A bei-sentence can express the passive voice, its structure being “subject＋被/叫/让＋object＋v. ＋...”, in which the subject is the patient of the action and the object the agent. The object following “被” can be left out, while the object after “叫” or “让” cannot. The negative adverbs and modal verbs should precede “被” if there are any.

例如 Example

（1）桃子**被**我吃了。

（2）杯子**被**打碎了。

（3）问题还没有**被**解决。

（4）大吃小，小**被**吃。（电影原句）

2 疑问代词活用

汉语中可用“谁”“什么”“怎么”“哪里/哪儿”等疑问代词代替某个范围内的每一个对象，它们都有相同的情况，没有例外。经常和“都”连用。

In Chinese, interrogative pronouns such as “谁”“什么”“怎么” and “哪里/哪儿” can be used to refer to every member in a certain scope, indicating all of them are the same in a certain way without exception. Often used together with “都”.

例如 Example

（1）她又会唱歌又会跳舞，**谁都**喜欢她。

（2）我生病了，**什么都**不想吃。

（3）只要有骨气，不吹牛，不打架，努力读书，就算穷，到**哪里都**会受到尊敬的。（电影原句）

综合练习 Comprehensive Exercises

一、选择恰当的词语填空并朗读 Choose the Proper Words to Fill in the Blanks and Read the Sentences Aloud

碰　穷　当　尊敬　方面

❶ 我想________一个足球明星。

❷ 这本书是哪________的？

❸ 因为没有工作，所以他现在很________。

❹ 中国人非常________父母。

❺ 他不小心________到了我。

二、听后重复句子 Repeat after Listening

三、判断对错 Ture or False

❶ 妮可·基特曼片酬不高。（　）

❷ 蛋挞头的志愿是做小企业家。（　）

❸ 周小狄觉得做穷人也很好。（　）

❹ 周爸爸告诉周小狄不要吹牛和打架。（　）

四、连词成句 Rearrange the Words or Phrases to Make Sentences

❶ 哥哥　了　牛奶　喝完　被 →

❷ 欢迎　受到　的　他　了　大家 →

❸ 有钱　不能　就算　买　也 →

❹ 喜欢　吃　我　什么　都 →

五、看图造句 Make Sentences According to the Pictures

放　　　　　　努力

______________　　______________

六、回答问题 Answer the Questions

❶ 蛋挞头的志愿是什么？

❷ 你觉得周小狄的志愿怎么样？

七、角色配音 Role Play

三人一组，分别扮演曹主任、蛋挞头和周小狄。

八、中文脱口秀 Chinese Talk Show（1.5 分钟）

你的志愿是什么？为什么？

提示：作家、画家、艺术家、记者、翻译、演员、歌手、设计师等。

文化知识 Cultural Knowledge

中国的新兴职业：网络主播
A New Career in China：Network Anchor

网络主播是一种新兴职业，指在互联网节目或活动中担当主持，主要有娱乐主播、游戏主播、电商主播等。娱乐主播通常有一定的才艺，比如唱歌、跳舞、演奏乐器等，游戏主播通过玩或讲解电子游戏吸引观看者，这两种主播主要通过获得的关注量和观看者送的虚拟礼物（也称为“打赏”）来取得收入。电商主播为观众展示和推荐商品（也称为“带货”），价格一般比市场价低。

Network anchor is a new profession, refers to the person who acts as the host in Internet programs or activities, mainly including entertainment anchor, game anchor, e-commerce anchor, etc. Entertainment anchors usually have certain talents, such as singing, dancing, playing musical instruments and so on. Game anchors engage viewers by playing or explaining video games. Both of these make money mainly from the amount of attention they receive and virtual gifts from viewers which also known as “tips”. E-commerce anchors show and recommend products to audience, also known as “live commerce”, and the price is usually lower than the market price.

第三课　课间 Between Classes

（电影片段 04：54—07：31）

生词 Words/Phrases

1. 超级	chāojí	adj.	super
2. 玩具	wánjù	n.	toy
3. 长江	Cháng Jiāng	n.	Yangtze River
4. 科学家	kēxuéjiā	n.	scientist
5. 共同	gòngtóng	adv. /adj.	together; common
6. 研究	yánjiū	v.	to research, to study
7. 世界	shìjiè	n.	world
8. 另外	lìngwài	pron. /conj.	other; besides, in addition
8. 总统	zǒngtǒng	n.	president
9. 干吗	gànmá	pron.	what to do; why
10. 站	zhàn	v.	to stand
11. 矮	ǎi	adj.	short
12. 成	chéng	v.	used before a complement of result; to become
13. 样子	yàngzi	n.	look, appearance
14. 有用	yǒuyòng	adj.	useful, helpful
15. 啦	la	part.	combination of the sound of 了 and 啊, expressing exclamation, interrogation, etc.
16. 素质	sùzhì	n.	quality
17. 低	dī	adj.	low
18. 才	cái	adv.	just
19. 吓	xià	v.	to frighten, to scare

20. 死	sǐ	v./adj.	to die; dead
21. 警察	jǐngchá	n.	police
22. 枪毙	qiāngbì	v.	to execute by shooting
23. 怪物	guàiwu	n.	monster, freak
24. 欺负	qīfu	v.	to bully
25. 英雄	yīngxióng	n.	hero
26. 理	lǐ	v.	to respond
27. 穷鬼	qióngguǐ	n.	pauper, the poor

语法点 Grammar Notes

1 "越来越"

"越来越"的后边加上形容词或心理动词，表示随着时间的推移程度上发生的变化。形容词或心理动词前边都不能再加程度副词。

Followed by an adjective or a mental verb, "越来越" indicates the change in degree occurs as time passes by. No adverb of degree is used before the adjective or mental verb.

例如 Example

(1) 来中国半年了，我的朋友**越来越**多。

(2) 他**越来越**喜欢看书。

(3) 妈妈做的饭**越来越**好吃。

(4) 为什么现在的学生的素质是**越来越**低?(电影原句)

2 动词重叠

动词的重叠形式用来表达短时间、少量、轻微、尝试的意思，语气比较轻松、随便，多用于口语中。

The reduplicative form of a verb indicates a short time, a small quantity, a slight degree or an attempt, conveying a relaxed and casual mood. It is often used in spoken Chinese.

例如 Example

v.	v. v.	v. 一 v.	v. 了 v.
说	说说	说一说	说了说
看	看看	看一看	看了看
听	听听	听一听	听了听
学习	学习学习	/	学习了学习
准备	准备准备	/	准备了准备
运动	运动运动	/	运动了运动

3 时间副词"就"

时间副词"就"可放在动词前做状语，强调说话人认为事情发生得早、进行得快或顺利。

The adverb of time "就" can be used as an adverbial modifier before a verb, indicates that in the speaker's opinion, something happened early, or went on fast and well.

例如 Example

（1）我七点**就**来教室了。

（2）他正在路上，十分钟**就**到。

（3）他十六岁**就**上大学了。

（4）你才几岁**就**长得那么大块？（电影原句）

综合练习 Comprehensive Exercises

一、选择恰当的词语填空并朗读 Choose the Proper Words to Fill in the Blanks and Read the Sentences Aloud

低　样子　站　理　另外

❶ 我和________两个同学都感冒了。

❷ 请你________在那边。

❸ 妹妹笑的________很可爱。

❹ 今天气温有点儿________。

❺ 她已经几天没________我了。

二、听后重复句子 Repeat after Listening

三、判断对错 Ture or False

❶ 蛋挞头说长江一号是三国的科学家研究出来的。　（　　）

❷ 长江一号在世界上只有两个。　（　　）

❸ 美娇长得不高也不胖。　（　　）

❹ 蛋挞头经常欺负同学。　（　　）

四、连词成句 Rearrange the Words or Phrases to Make Sentences

❶ 想　我　旅游　越来越　去 →

❷ 说一说　事情　请　你　这件 →

❸ 他　就　写完了　十分钟　作业 →

❹ 要　什么　妹妹　玩具　都 →

五、看图造句 Make Sentences According to the Pictures

矮

素质

______________　______________

六、回答问题 Answer the Questions

❶ 周爸爸在哪里吃饭？

❷ 美娇为什么哭？

七、中文脱口秀 Chinese Talk Show（1.5 分钟）

你记得小时候玩过什么玩具吗？

提示：娃娃、积木、拼图、魔方、机器人等。

文化知识 Cultural Knowledge

中国玩具之都

The Toy Capital of China

广东省汕头市澄海区被称为“中国玩具之都”和“世界玩具工厂”。澄海区面积大约 380 平方公里，有上万家玩具企业，工作人员十几万人，玩具产品畅销海内外，年产值达到数百亿元。玩具产品畅销海内外，年产值达到数百亿元。现在，澄海的玩具产业向“玩具 + 动漫 + 游戏 + 影视”的新模式转型，向高端化、品牌化、智能化的方向发展。

Chenghai District, Shantou City, Guangdong Province, is known as “the toy capital of China” and “the toy factory of the world”. Chenghai covers an area of about 380 square kilometers, with tens of thousands of toy enterprises and more than 100,000 employees. Toy products sell well at home and abroad, and the annual output value reaches tens of billions of yuan. Now, Chenghai’s toy industry develop to “toys & animation & games & film and television” new mode of transformation to a high-end, branded, intelligent direction.

汉语成语 Chinese Idiom

"奇形怪状"意为"奇怪的、不同一般的形状"。

"奇形怪状"means a grotesque appearance or shape.

例如 Example

这棵树长得奇形怪状。

第四课　罚站 Stand for a Punishment

（电影片段 07：32—08：55）

生词 Words/Phrases

1. 罚站	fázhàn	v.	to stand for a punishment
2. 带	dài	v.	to take along，to bring
3. 其实	qíshí	adv.	actually
4. 只	zhǐ / zhī	adv. /m.	only，solely；used for certain animals
5. 故意	gùyì	adv.	intentionally，on purpose
6. 换	huàn	v.	to change，to substitute
7. 而已	éryǐ	part.	nothing more，only
8. 陪	péi	v.	to accompany
9. 鞋	xié	n.	shoe
10. 破	pò	adj.	broken，torn
11. 所有	suǒyǒu	adj.	all
12. 捡	jiǎn	v.	to pick up，to collect
13. 呀	ya	part.	a variant of the interjection 啊
14. 不过	búguò	conj.	but，yet
15. 双	shuāng	m.	pair
16. 体育	tǐyù	n.	P. E. ，sports
17. 永远	yǒngyuǎn	adv.	forever

语法点 Grammar Notes

1 "的"字短语

代词、名词、动词、形容词和"的"可以组成相当于省略中心语的名词短语。

"的" can be used after a pronoun, a noun, a verb or an adjective to form a phrase which is equivalent to a nominal phrase with its headword omitted.

例如 Example

(1) 这本书是**我的**。

(2) 那个**黄色的**很便宜。

(3) 我去买一点儿**吃的**。

(4) 我所有的鞋都是**破的**。(电影原句)

2 "是……的"句

在已经知道事情发生的情况下，可以用"是……的"句强调动作的发出者和事情发生的时间、地点、方式，否定形式在"是"前加"不"。

When the occurrence of something is known, "是……的" can be used to emphasize the agent of the action, and when, where, in which manner it occurred. In the negative form, "不" is added before "是".

例如 Example

(1) 香蕉**是**妈妈买回来**的**。

(2) 我**是**昨天来**的**。

(3) 这**不是**在北京买**的**。

(4) 我所有的鞋都是破的，都**是**我爸爸从外面捡回来**的**。(电影原句)

综合练习 Comprehensive Exercises

一、选择恰当的词语填空并朗读 Choose the Proper Words to Fill in the Blanks and Read the Sentences Aloud

而已　不过　换　故意　破

❶ 我________没带笔。

❷ 她只是一个孩子________。

3 书包被弟弟弄________了。
4 他想去旅行，________没有时间。
5 请问银行在哪儿？我要________一些人民币。

二、听后重复句子 Repeat after Listening

三、判断对错 Ture or False
1 美娇也被罚站了。（　　）
2 美娇没带运动鞋。（　　）
3 周小狄所有的鞋都是他爸爸买的。（　　）
4 周小狄想要一双新的运动鞋。（　　）

四、连词成句 Rearrange the Words or Phrases to Make Sentences
1 很　绿色　那件　难看　的→
2 这个　不是　的　房间　她→
3 是　飞机票　买　爸爸　的→
4 我　其实　唱歌　不会→

五、看图造句 Make Sentences According to the Pictures

捡　　　　　　陪

______________　　______________

六、回答问题 Answer the Questions

❶ 美娇为什么被罚站？

❷ 周小狄的鞋是哪里来的？

七、角色配音 Role Play

两人一组，分别扮演美娇和周小狄。

八、中文脱口秀 Chinese Talk Show（1.5 分钟）

你喜欢和擅长什么体育运动？

提示：滑雪、滑冰、打羽毛球、打台球、射箭等。

文化知识 Cultural Knowledge

中国的“国球”：乒乓球
China's National Game: Table Tennis

乒乓球被称为中国的“国球”，是大众非常喜爱的体育项目，也是中国队在奥运会和世界比赛中的夺冠热点。1959 年，容国团在第二十五届世界乒乓球锦标赛上为中国获得世界体育比赛中第一个世界冠军。目前中国的乒乓球项目在世界上排名第一，已经有一百多名中国运动员获得过世界乒乓球冠军，比如邓亚萍、刘国梁、孔令辉、王楠、马琳、张怡宁、王励勤、马龙、张继科、许昕、孙颖莎等。中国乒乓球协会的官方网站是 https://www.ctta.cn/。

Table tennis, known as China's "national game", is a popular sport and a hot spot for the Chinese team to win gold medals in the Olympic Games and world competitions. In 1959, Rong Guotuan won the first world championship in world sport for China at the 25th World Table Tennis Championships. At present, China ranks first place in table tennis events around the world. More than 100 Chinese athletes have won world table tennis championships, such as Deng Yaping, Liu Guoliang, Kong Linghui, Wang Nan, Ma Lin, Zhang Yining, Wang Liqin, Ma Long, Zhang Jike, Xu Xin, Sun Yingsha and so on. The official website of the Chinese Table Tennis Association is https://www.ctta.cn/.

第五课　在工地 At Construction Site

(电影片段 08：56—10：47)

生词 Words/Phrases

1. 劲（儿）	jìn（r）	n.	strength
2. 歇	xiē	v.	to rest，to take a rest
3. 老板	lǎobǎn	n.	boss，employer
4. 风扇	fēngshàn	n.	electric fan
5. 盖	gài	v.	to build；to cover
6. 不如	bùrú	v.	to be not as good as，to be inferior to
7. 先	xiān	adv.	first，in advance
8. 还	huán	v.	to return
9. 老婆	lǎopo	n.	wife
10. 费	fèi	n.	cost
11. 殡葬	bìnzàng	n.	funeral
12. 副	fù	m.	pair；set
13. 德行	déxing	n.	appearance
14. 一辈子	yībèizi	n.	all one's life
15. 供	gòng	v.	to supply
16. 贵族	guìzú	n.	noble
17. 普通	pǔtōng	adj.	common
18. 分别	fēnbié	n. /adv.	difference；respectively
19. 将来	jiānglái	n.	future
20. 能力	nénglì	n.	ability，competence
21. 嘛	ma	part.	to indicate that the reason is obvious
22. 强	qiáng	adj.	strong

23. 散工	sǎngōng	n.	casual laborer
24. 凭	píng	v. /prep.	to rely on; on the basis of
25. 顶	dǐng	v. /n.	to be qualified; to go against; top
26. 座	zuò	m.	used for buildings, bridges, mountains, etc.
27. 凿	záo	v.	to chisel
28. 水泥	shuǐní	n.	cement
29. 地	dì	n.	ground

语法点 Grammar Notes

1 可能补语

汉语中用"动词＋得＋补语"或"动词＋不＋补语"表示能否实现某种结果或达到某种目的。"动词＋得＋补语"是肯定形式，"动词＋不＋补语"是否定形式。"得"后的补语常常是结果补语、趋向补语。疑问形式为"动词＋得＋补语＋动词＋不＋补语"或"动词＋得＋补语＋吗"。

In Chinese, "v. ＋得＋complements" or " v. ＋不＋complements" can be used to indicate whether or not a result can be obtained or a goal be reached. "v. ＋得＋complements" is the positive form, and "v. ＋不＋complements" is the negative form. The complements used in this structure are usually complements of result or direction. The interrogative form is "v. ＋得＋complements＋v. ＋不＋complements" or "v. ＋得＋complements＋吗".

例如 Example

(1) 我只欠他 500 块钱，我**还得完**。

(2) 他不饿，**吃不完**这碗米饭。

(3) 你**看得清看不清**？/你**看得清**吗？

(4) 因为这几天好热，我儿子他都**睡不好**。(电影原句)

2 连词"那"

"那"放在句首表示依据上文的意思得出结果或做出的判断。

Used at the beginning of a sentence, "那" indicates the result obtained or judgment made based on what has been said previously.

例如 Example

（1）A：明天我不想去看电影了。

　　B：**那**我也不去了。

（2）A：他的身体很好。

　　B：**那**也要经常运动。

（3）A：也不是，不过是想让他读好一点，不想他将来跟我一样嘛。

　　B：**那**你也要有能力才行嘛。（电影原句）

综合练习 Comprehensive Exercises

一、选择恰当的词语填空并朗读 Choose the Proper Words to Fill in the Blanks and Read the Sentences Aloud

不如　座　凭　将来　费

❶ 我觉得可乐________芬达好喝。

❷ 他每年的学________是一万元。

❸ ________我要当一名警察。

❹ ________他的努力，一定能考上大学。

❺ 前面有一________商场。

二、听后重复句子 Repeat after Listening

三、判断对错 Ture or False

❶ 这几天周小狄睡得很好。　（　）

❷ 周小狄读的是普通学校。　（　）

❸ 周爸爸不希望周小狄将来和自己一样。　（　）

❹ 老板觉得周爸爸没有能力。　（　）

四、连词成句 Rearrange the Words or Phrases to Make Sentences

1. 教室　我　不　找　到 →
2. 听得懂　这个　你　问题　听不懂 →
3. 父母　孩子　挣钱　读书　供 →
4. 还给　下个　自行车　星期　你 →

五、看图造句 Make Sentences According to the Pictures

劲（儿）

____

盖

____

六、回答问题 Answer the Questions

1. 周爸爸为什么要让周小狄读贵族学校？
2. 老板为什么觉得周爸爸供不起周小狄读贵族学校？

七、角色配音 Role Play

两人一组，分别扮演周爸爸和老板。

八、中文脱口秀 Chinese Talk Show（1.5 分钟）

以后你会让自己的孩子读普通学校还是贵族学校？

提示：学费、私立、公立、设施等。

文化知识 Cultural Knowledge

中国的农民工
Migrant Workers in China

农民工也称民工、进城务工人员，是指为用人单位提供劳动的农村居民，是在中国改革开放和工业化、城镇化进程中出现的新型劳动群体。农民工主要从事非农业产业，比如建筑工人、流水线工人、外卖员、保安等。有的农民工在农闲时外出打工，有的长期在城市就业，他们已经成为产业工人的重要组成部分。根据中国国家统计局发布的数据，2021 年中国农民工总数近 3 亿人。

Migrant workers, also known as peasant-workers, refer to rural residents who provide labor for employers and are a new type of labor group emerging in the process of China's reform and opening-up, industrialization and urbanization. Migrant workers are mainly employed in non-agricultural industries, such as construction workers, assembly line workers, food delivery workers and security guards. Some migrant workers go out to work in the slack time of the farm, some long-term employment in the city, they have become an important part of the industrial workers. According to data released by China's National Bureau of Statistics, the total number of migrant workers in China in 2021 was nearly 300 million.

第六课　旧风扇 An Old Fan

（电影片段 10：48—14：50）

生词 Words/Phrases

1. 肚子	dùzi	n.	belly，stomach
2. 饿	è	adj.	hungry
3. 退	tuì	v.	to go back
4. 转	zhuǎn	v.	to turn，to shift
5. 还是	háishi	conj.	or
6. 假	jiǎ	adj.	false，fake
7. 终于	zhōngyú	adv.	finally
8. 扇	shàn	n.	fan
9. 旧	jiù	adj.	old，used，worn
10. 耍	shuǎ	v.	to cheat，to play，to behave (in an unsavory manner)
11. 好端端	hǎoduānduān	adj.	in good condition，when everything is all right
12. 爆	bào	v.	to explode，to burst
13. 机灵	jīling	adj.	smart
14. 乱	luàn	adv. /adj.	random；disordered；confused
15. 偷	tōu	v.	to steal
16. 抢	qiǎng	v.	to rob
17. 属于	shǔyú	v.	to belong to
18. 念	niàn	v.	to read
19. 时代	shídài	n.	era，age，epoch
20. 补	bǔ	v.	to repair，to patch
21. 最好	zuìhǎo	adv.	had better

22. 不然	bùrán	conj.	or else, otherwise
23. 尽力	jìn lì	v.	to try one's best
24. 进步	jìnbù	n. /v.	progress; to make a progress

语法点 Grammar Notes

1 概数“几”

“几”可以表示10以内的不定个数，后边要有量词。“十几”表示大于10小于20的数字，“几十”表示大于20小于100的数字。

“几” indicates an indefinite number less than 10, “十几” indicates a number greater than 10 but less than 20, “几十” indicates a number greater than 20 while less than 100.

例如 Example

（1）我买了**几**本书。

（2）他有**十几**块钱，不到二十。

（3）教室里有**几十**个人。

（4）好**几十**块钱呢这旧风扇！（电影原句）

2 “是不是”

如果提问的人对某个事实或者情况有比较肯定的估计，可以用“是不是”进行提问。“是不是”一般用在谓语前面，也可以用在句首或者句尾。

If one raises a question and is somehow certain about a fact or situation, they can use “是不是” to confirm their guess. “是不是” is usually used before the predicate, or at the beginning or end of a sentence.

例如 Example

（1）周六你**是不是**要去游泳？

（2）明天国庆节，**是不是**我们休息？

（3）他下个月去中国，**是不是**？

（4）你**是不是**又给人要了？（电影原句）

3 “虽然……但是……”

“虽然……但是……”连接两个分句，构成转折关系。

The conjunctions “虽然……但是……” connect two clauses, forming a complex sentence indicating an adversative relation.

例如 Example

（1）**虽然**今天是晴天，**但是**很冷。

（2）**虽然**有些人很有钱，**但是**并不快乐。

（3）他**虽然**穷，**但是**很有骨气。

（4）我们**虽然**穷，**但（是）**不乱说脏话。（电影原句）

4 离合词

离合词是汉语特有的语法现象，它是既可以分开又可以合用的词语，兼有单词和词组的特征。离合词中间的插入成分包括动态助词“着”“了”“过”，结构助词“的”，数量短语，时量补语，动量补语，结果补语，可能补语，限定性定语等。

Separable words form a unique phenomenon in Chinese, they are a special kind of words that can be used either separately or as an entire unit. A separable word shows the properties of both word and phrase. Inserted components including aspect particles “着”“了”“过”, structural particles “的”, numeral-classifier phrases, complements of duration/frequency/result/possibility, descriptive or limiting attributes, etc.

例如 Example

（1）今天我**吃了两顿饭**。

（2）我和他**见过面**。

（3）我经常**洗冷水澡**。

（4）**吃完饭**再吃水果。（电影原句）

综合练习 Comprehensive Exercises

一、选择恰当的词语填空并朗读 Choose the Proper Words to Fill in the Blanks and Read the Sentences Aloud

假　进步　属于　饿　还是

❶ 我没吃早饭，现在肚子________了。

❷ 买橙子________买梨？

❸ 要说真话，不要说________话。

❹ 成功________我们。

❺ 他的汉语________不小。

二、听后重复句子 Repeat after Listening

三、判断对错 Ture or False

1. 电风扇是周爸爸捡回来的。 ( )
2. 周爸爸告诉周小狄不能去偷、去抢。 ( )
3. 周爸爸小时候不能上学。 ( )
4. 周爸爸又捡了一双运动鞋。 ( )

四、连词成句 Rearrange the Words or Phrases to Make Sentences

1. 打破了 他 十几 鸡蛋 个 →
2. 歌 了 姐姐 三首 唱 →
3. 你 出去 想 玩 是不是 →
4. 生病 又 上个月 她 了 →

五、看图造句 Make Sentences According to the Pictures

乱

____

偷

____

六、回答问题 Answer the Questions

1. 旧电风扇买的时候怎么样?
2. 如果周小狄的衣服和鞋破了怎么办?

七、角色配音 Role Play

两人一组，分别扮演周爸爸和周小狄。

八、中文脱口秀 Chinese Talk Show（1.5 分钟）

周爸爸是怎么教育儿子的?

文化知识 Cultural Knowledge

中国人重视教育的传统

The Tradition of Appreciating Education

中华民族自古以来就是非常注重教育的民族。两千多年前的春秋时期，中国著名的思想家、教育家、儒家学派创始人孔子提倡“有教无类”，让普通平民也能接受教育；战国时期，孟子的母亲为了让孟子有良好的学习环境，搬了三次家，留下了“孟母三迁”的故事。从古至今，中国人一直相信学习能够改变命运，中国的父母们通常都会尽力为子女提供好的学习环境和条件，子女的教育支出占所有家庭支出的很大比例。重视教育是中国人的文化基因之一。

Since ancient times, Chinese people have attached great importance to education. More than 2,000 years ago, in the Spring and Autumn Period, Confucius, a famous Chinese thinker, who is the educator and founder of the Confucian School, advocated the principle of “education without discrimination” so that ordinary people could receive education. During the Warring States Period, Mencius' mother moved three times in order to provide him a good learning environment. In all ages, Chinese people have always believed that learning can change their destiny. Chinese parents usually try their best to provide good learning environment and conditions for their children, whose education expenses account for a large proportion of all family expenditures. Attaching importance to education is one of the cultural genes of the Chinese people.

第七课　在玩具店 In Toy Shop

（电影片段 14：51—18：03）

生词 Words/Phrases

1. 最近	zuìjìn	adv.	lately，recently
2. 关于	guānyú	prep.	about，regarding
3. 飞行	fēixíng	v.	to fly
4. 物体	wùtǐ	n.	object
5. 简称	jiǎnchēng	v. /n.	for short；abbreviation
6. 报道	bàodào	v. /n.	to report；report
7. 动画片	dònghuàpiàn	n.	animated cartoon
8. 马上	mǎshàng	adv.	immediately，at once
9. 当时	dāngshí	n.	then，at that time
10. 情况	qíngkuàng	n.	situation，circumstance
11. 飞碟	fēidié	n.	flying saucer (UFO)
12. 嗖	sōu	onom.	whoosh
13. 详细	xiángxì	adj.	detailed
14. 摇晃	yáohuàng	v. /adj.	to shake；shaky
15. 怀疑	huáiyí	v.	to suspect，to doubt
16. 撞	zhuàng	v.	to bump against
17. 好像	hǎoxiàng	adv.	as if
18. 坏	huài	adj.	bad，broken
19. 拍	pāi	v.	to take (a photo)，to shoot (a video)
20. 照片	zhàopiàn	n.	photo
21. 相机	xiàngjī	n.	camera
22. 玩意儿	wányìr	n.	thing，stuff

23. 至于	zhìyú	prep.	as for, as to
24. 牌子	páizi	n.	brand
25. 方便	fāngbiàn	adj.	convenient
26. 发	fā	v.	to send out, to launch
27. 声响	shēngxiǎng	n.	sound, voice
28. 工资	gōngzī	n.	pay, salary
29. 求	qiú	v.	to beg
30. 功能	gōngnéng	n.	function

语法点 Grammar Notes

1 "一下"

"一下"用在动词后，表示一次短暂的动作，相当于动词重叠，宾语可以省略。

"一下" is used after a verb to indicate a short action, similar to the reduplicative form of a verb. The object of the verb can be omitted.

例如 Example

（1）这是什么？我看**一下**。

（2）你休息**一下**，五分钟之后再运动。

（3）那道题很难，我问**一下**老师。

（4）马上来，你等**一下**嘛。（电影原句）

2 形容词重叠

汉语中形容词重叠表示程度深，常用来描述人或事物的特征。

In Chinese, reduplication of adjectives can describe the characteristics of a person or thing, indicating a deep degree.

例如 Example

（1）小草**绿绿的**。

（2）他的眼睛**大大的**。

（3）今天她穿得**漂漂亮亮的**。

（4）那个飞碟会飞的，但是飞得**摇摇晃晃的**。（电影原句）

3 动态助词“过”

动词后加上动态助词“过”，一般用来表示过去的经历，这些动作行为没有持续到现在。在动词前边加“没有”表示否定，在句尾加“吗”“没有”表示疑问。

A verb followed by the aspect particle “过” usually indicates a past experience action which hasn't lasted to the present. In the negative form, “没有” is added before the verb. In the interrogative form, “吗” “没有” is added at the end of the sentence.

例如 Example

（1）我听**过**这首歌，你听**过**吗？

（2）他没有去**过**中国。

（3）你看**过**电影《长江七号》没有？

（4）我怀疑它撞**过**。（电影原句）

综合练习 Comprehensive Exercises

一、选择恰当的词语填空并朗读 Choose the Proper Words to Fill in the Blanks and Read the Sentences Aloud

方便　关于　工资　怀疑　情况

1. ________这个词的意思，你们都懂了吗？
2. 今天上课的________怎么样？
3. 我________那件事是他做的。
4. 超市离这里不远，买东西很________。
5. 这个月的________还没发。

二、听后重复句子 Repeat after Listening

三、判断对错 Ture or False

❶ 有人给飞碟拍了照片。　(　　)

❷ 飞碟可能撞坏了。　(　　)

❸ 周小狄非常想要长江一号。　(　　)

❹ 周爸爸说下个月再买长江一号。　(　　)

四、连词成句 Rearrange the Words or Phrases to Make Sentences

❶ 机场　了　马上　我们　要到 →

❷ 那里　我　一下　去　休息 →

❸ 她　过　没有　绿茶　喝 →

❹ 的　手　他的　黑黑 →

五、看图造句 Make Sentences According to the Pictures

撞

____

牌子

____

六、回答问题 Answer the Questions

❶ 那个飞碟是怎么飞的?

❷ 周爸爸为什么不给周小狄买长江一号?

七、角色配音 Role Play

四人一组，分别扮演记者、目击者、周爸爸和周小狄。

八、中文脱口秀 Chinese Talk Show（1.5 分钟）

你对飞碟和外星人有什么看法？

提示：地球、宇宙、人类、生命、科技、科幻电影等。

文化知识 Cultural Knowledge

中国的航天事业

China's Space Industry

14 世纪末，明朝的万户坐在绑着火箭的椅子上，尝试利用火箭的推力飞上天空，但是没有成功。中国于 1970 年发射了第一颗人造地球卫星东方红一号，2003 年神舟五号载人飞船升空，杨利伟成为第一个进入太空的中国公民。2007 年中国首颗探月卫星嫦娥一号升空，2012 年刘洋成了中国第一位进入太空的女航天员，2020 年中国首颗火星探测器天问一号发射。中国的系列运载火箭叫作“长征”，中国的空间站叫作“天宫”。

In the late 14th century, Wanhu of the Ming Dynasty, sitting on a chair strapped to a rockets he made, tried unsuccessfully to use the thrust of rockets to fly into the sky. In 1970, China launched its first man-made earth satellite Dongfanghong-1. When Shenzhou V manned spacecraft has been launched in 2003, Yang Liwei became the first Chinese citizen to go into space. In 2007, Chang'e-1, China's first lunar probe, was launched. In 2012, Liu Yang became China's first female astronaut. In 2020, China's first Mars probe, Tianwen-1, was launched. China's launch vehicles are called Long March and its space station is called Tiangong.

第八课　周爸爸和袁老师 Mr. Zhou and Teacher Yuan

(电影片段 18：04—19：25)

生词 Words/Phrases

1. 哭	kū	v.	to cry
2. 乖	guāi	adj.	obedient，well-behaved
3. 挺	tǐng	adv.	quite，rather
4. 脾气	píqi	n.	temper，disposition
5. 刚好	gānghǎo	adv.	by coincidence
6. 一直	yīzhí	adv.	all the time
7. 家访	jiāfǎng	v.	to visit the parents of school-children
8. 比较	bǐjiào	adv.	fairly，rather
9. 教育	jiàoyù	v./n.	to educate；education
10. 单	dān	adv.	only，solely
11. 靠	kào	v.	to rely on，to depend on；to lean against
12. 沟通	gōutōng	v.	to communicate

语法点 Grammar Notes

1 语气副词“还”

“还”表示动作或状态的延续。另外“还＋形容词”表示勉强过得去。

“还” indicates the continuation of an action or a state. In addition，the structure “还＋adj.” means that something is passable or acceptable.

例如 Example

(1) 已经下午两点了，你怎么**还**没吃午饭？

（2）现在是上午十点，弟弟**还**在睡觉。

（3）爷爷很瘦，但是身体**还**可以/**还**行。

（4）他刚刚**还**在发脾气。（电影原句）

2 介词“对”

介词“对”可以表示人和人、人和事物、事物和事物之间的对待关系。

The preposition “对” can indicate a subject-target relation between people or things.

例如 Example

（1）哥哥**对**我很好，经常给我买礼物。

（2）看中国电影**对**学习汉语有帮助。

（3）我很想很想多和你做一些沟通，这样**对**他也比较好。（电影原句）

综合练习 Comprehensive Exercises

一、选择恰当的词语填空并朗读 Choose the Proper Words to Fill in the Blanks and Read the Sentences Aloud

教育　哭　脾气　挺　靠

❶ 她________得很伤心。

❷ 机场离学校________远。

❸ 他________不好，经常大吼大叫。

❹ 每个人都应该受________。

❺ 中国有句老话：“在家________父母，出门________朋友。”

二、听后重复句子 Repeat after Listening

三、判断对错 Ture or False

❶ 这是袁老师和周爸爸第一次见面。（　　）

❷ 袁老师说周小狄在学校不乖。（　　）

❸ 因为周爸爸很忙，所以袁老师没有去做家访。（　　）

❹ 周爸爸不想和袁老师沟通。（　　）

四、连词成句 Rearrange the Words or Phrases to Make Sentences

❶ 做　作业　还没　他　完 →

❷ 看手机　长时间　不好　对　眼睛 →

❸ 这次　比较　的　简单　考试 →

❹ 下雨　外面　在　一直 →

五、看图造句 Make Sentences According to the Pictures

一直

发脾气

______________________　　______________________

六、回答问题 Answer the Questions

❶ 周小狄为什么哭？

❷ 袁老师为什么想去周小狄家做家访？

七、角色配音 Role Play

两人一组，分别扮演袁老师和周爸爸。

八、中文脱口秀 Chinese Talk Show（1.5 分钟）

你的第一位汉语老师是什么样的人？

提示：姓名、年龄、长相、性格、故事等。

文化知识 Cultural Knowledge

中国学校的家访制度

Home Visiting System in Chinese School

除了召开家长会和请家长来学校，家访也是中国教师的工作之一，可存在于各个教育阶段，一般是指班主任去学生家里和家长进行谈话，沟通关于学生学习、在校表现等方面的情况，争取家长相应的配合和支持。通过家访，教师可以更真实、更全面地了解每一个学生的家庭状况、学习环境和在家的表现，了解家长的希望、要求以及教育方法等，同时也可以帮助家长树立正确的教育理念、解决家庭教育中的一些问题，使家长主动参与到学校的教育教学管理中来。

In addition to holding parents' meetings and inviting parents to school, home visiting is also one of the job duties of Chinese teachers, which exists in all stages of education. In general, it means that the head teacher goes to the students' home to talk with their parents about the students' study and performance for the corresponding cooperation and supporting of parents. By this way, teachers can more truly, more fully understand each student's family situation, learning environment and performance at home, know the parents' goals, requirements and education methods, etc. At the same time it also can help parents to set up the correct education concepts, solve some problems in family education, make the parents actively participate in school education and teaching management.

第九课　奇怪的绿球 A Strange Green Ball

(电影片段 19：26—24：53)

生词 Words/Phrases

1. 头	tóu	n.	head
2. 厉害	lìhai	adj.	awesome，serious
3. 扔	rēng	v.	to throw away
4. 掉	diào	v.	used after certain verbs，indicating the result of an action
5. 算了	suànle	part.	forget it，never mind，let it be
6. 加班	jiā bān	v.	to work overtime
7. 一定	yīdìng	adv.	definitely，certainly
8. 垃圾	lājī	n.	rubbish，garbage
9. 桶	tǒng	n.	barrel，bucket
10.（允）许	（yǔn）xǔ	v.	to allow，to permit
11.（要）不然	（yào）bùrán	conj.	otherwise，or else

语法点 Grammar Notes

1 "把"字句＋结果/趋向补语

表达对确定的人或事物产生某种结果或发生位置上的改变，结构为"A 把 B＋动词＋结果/趋向补语"。

The structure "A 把 B＋v.＋complement of result/direction" can be used to indicate an action which is done on a definite person or thing and has brought a result to or has changed the position of the person or thing.

例如 Example

（1）妻子把饭做好了。

（2）苹果在冰箱里，请你把它拿出来。

（3）把头转过来。（电影原句）

2 “比”字句

用“比”表示比较的句子叫“比”字句，形式为“A 比 B＋形容词”，可在形容词后用具体数量表示具体差别，用“一点儿/一些”表示差别不大，用“多了/得多”表示差别大。否定形式为“A 没有 B＋形容词”。如果动词带状态补语，形式为“A 比 B＋动词＋得＋形容词”或“A＋动词＋得＋比 B＋形容词”。

A “比” sentence is a sentence using “比” to make a comparison, its structure being “A 比 B＋adj. ”, a specific number can be used after the adjective to specify the difference, and “一点儿/一些” can follow the adjective to indicate a slight difference, while “多了/得多” indicate a big difference. The negative form is “A 没有 B＋adj. ”. If a verb takes a complement of state, its structure being “A 比 B＋v. ＋得＋adj. ” or “A＋v. ＋得＋比 B＋adj. ”.

例如 Example

（1）我十六岁，他十八岁，他**比**我大（两岁）。

（2）姐姐**比**妹妹高（一点儿/一些/多了/得多）。

（3）昨天太热了，今天**没有**昨天热。

（4）我**比**他跑得快。/我跑得**比**他快。

（5）我有一个玩具，**比**长江一号更厉害。（电影原句）

3 动态助词“着”

动词加上动态助词“着”可以表示某种状态的持续，在这个动词前加“没（有）”表示否定，在句末加“没（有）”表示疑问。

A verb followed by the aspect particle “着” can indicate the continuation of a certain state. In the negative form, “没（有）” is added before the verb. In the interrogative form, “没（有）” is added at the end of the sentence.

例如 Example

（1）门没有开**着**，关**着**呢。

（2）你带**着**钱没有？

（3）你手里拿**着**什么东西啊？（电影原句）

综合练习 Comprehensive Exercises

一、选择恰当的词语填空并朗读 Choose the Proper Words to Fill in the Blanks and Read the Sentences Aloud

算了　一定　厉害　不然　允许

❶ 她打网球比我________。

❷ 这种车太贵，买不起，看一看________。

❸ 我________会帮助你。

❹ 爸爸不________他玩游戏。

❺ 起床吧，________迟到了。

二、听后重复句子 Repeat after Listening

三、判断对错 Ture or False

❶ 周爸爸看见了 UFO。（　）

❷ 小芬觉得长江七号很好玩。（　）

❸ 蛋挞头说长江七号是垃圾。（　）

❹ 周小狄说长江一号没有长江七号厉害。（　）

四、连词成句 Rearrange the Words or Phrases to Make Sentences

❶ 他　拿进　把　水果　房间　了 →

❷ 把　请　垃圾　这些　扔掉 →

❸ 比　火车票　一点儿　飞机票　便宜 →

❹ 着　刚才　站　他　没有 →

五、看图造句 Make Sentences According to the Pictures

比

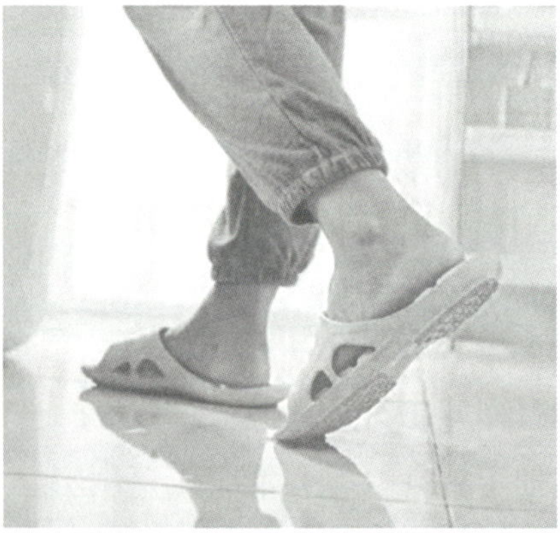

着

____________________ ____________________

六、回答问题 Answer the Questions

❶ 周爸爸是怎么找到那个绿球的？

❷ 周小狄为什么要打蛋挞头？

七、角色配音 Role Play

三人一组，分别扮演周小狄、小芬和蛋挞头。

八、中文脱口秀 Chinese Talk Show（1.5 分钟）

你现在喜欢玩什么？

提示：电脑游戏、手机游戏、桌面游戏、扑克、麻将等。

文化知识 Cultural Knowledge

长　江

The Changjiang River/The Yangtze River

长江发源于青藏高原，流经中国 11 个省级行政区，在上海崇明岛东部注入东海，流域面积达 180 万平方公里，约占中国陆地总面积的 1/5。长江全长 6397 千米，是亚洲第一长河，也是世界第三长河，仅次于非洲的尼罗河和南美洲的亚马孙河。长江和黄河都是中华民族的母亲河，具有重要的文化意义、生态意义和经济意义。

The Changjiang River/The Yangtze River originates from The Qinghai-Tibet Plateau, flows through 11 provincial-level administrative regions of China, and empties into the East China Sea in the east of Chongming Island in Shanghai. The Changjiang River covers an area of 1.8 million square kilometers, accounting for about one-fifth of China's total land area. With a total length of 6,397 kilometers, the Changjiang River is the longest river in Asia and the third longest in the world, after the Nile in Africa and the Amazon in South America. The Changjiang River and the Yellow River are both mother rivers of Chinese with great cultural, ecological and economic significance.

第十课　长江七号 CJ7

（电影片段 24：54—34：31）

生词 Words/Phrases

1. 遍	biàn	m.	(denoting an action from beginning to end) time
2. 长进	zhǎngjìn	v.	to make a progress, to improve
3. 逼	bī	v.	to force, to compel
4. 转移	zhuǎnyí	v.	to transfer, to shift
5. 话题	huàtí	n.	topic
6.（相）信	（xiāng）xìn	v.	to believe
7. 巴掌	bāzhang	n.	palm
8. 挂	guà	v.	to hang, to put up
9. 救	jiù	v.	to save, to rescue
10. 命	mìng	n.	life
11. 恐怖	kǒngbù	adj.	terrible, horrible
12. 吵	chǎo	v./adj.	to make a noise; noisy
13. 灯	dēng	n.	light, lamp
14. 像	xiàng	v.	to be like
15. 丢	diū	v.	to throw, to cast; to lose
16. 丸	wán	n.	bolus
17. 关	guān	v.	to lock, to close, to turn off
18. 骗	piàn	v.	to cheat, to deceive
19. 怕	pà	v.	to be afraid, to be scared
20. 敢	gǎn	v.	to dare
21. 调皮	tiáopí	adj.	naughty, mischievous

22. 星	xīng	n.	star, planet
23. 侵略	qīnlüè	v.	to invade, to aggress
24. 地球	dìqiú	n.	earth, globe
25. 尾巴	wěiba	n.	tail
26. 烂	làn	adj.	rotten, putrid
27. 新鲜	xīnxiān	adj.	fresh
28. 变魔术	biàn móshù	phr.	to perform magic tricks, to conjure
29. 甜	tián	adj.	sweet
30. 肯定	kěndìng	adv.	surely, certainly
31. 发财	fā cái	v.	to be rich

语法点 Grammar Notes

1 结果补语

一些动词或形容词可以放在动词后边，补充、说明动作的结果，它们叫作结果补语。在动词前加“没（有）”表示否定，句尾不能用“了”。表示疑问时，常在句尾加上“了没（有）”。

Some verbs or adjectives can be used after a verb to add remarks about the result of an action. They are called complements of result. “没（有）” is added before the verb to form the negative form of a complement of result, in which case “了” cannot appear at the end of the sentence. To form a question, “了没（有）” is often added at the end of the sentence.

例如 Example

（1）我**看见**他了，他在教室里。

（2）我没（有）**听到**他的话。

（3）时间到了，你**做完**题了没（有）？

（4）她**买好**飞机票了，下星期就回国。

（5）你看看，校服**破成**这个样子，明天怎么上学啊？（电影原句）

2 语气副词“好”

“好＋形容词”表示感叹语气，表示的确、实在，相当于“真＋形容词”。

The structure “好＋adj.” expresses an exclamatory mood, meaning “really” or “indeed", which is equivalent to "真＋adj. ".

例如 Example

（1）车里面**好**热，能开一下空调吗？

（2）这个女孩**好**漂亮，很像一个女明星。

（3）医院离饭店**好**远，有十公里。

（4）**好**怕！太恐怖了！（电影原句）

综合练习 Comprehensive Exercises

一、选择恰当的词语填空并朗读 Choose the Proper Words to Fill in the Blanks and Read the Sentences Aloud

遍　关　甜　挂　骗

1. 我读了三________课文。
2. 墙上________着一幅画。
3. 他没有________过别人。
4. 已经很晚了，________灯睡觉吧。
5. 这个草莓好________。

二、听后重复句子 Repeat after Listening

三、判断对错 Ture or False

1. 房间里有鬼。（　）
2. 周爸爸要补周小狄的校服。（　）
3. 周小狄被关在柜子里了。（　）
4. 长江七号能把烂苹果变新鲜。（　）

四、连词成句 Rearrange the Words or Phrases to Make Sentences

❶ 跳舞 的 她 好美 样子 →

❷ 到 工作 没有 哥哥 找 →

❸ 我的 很大 有 汉语 长进 →

❹ 他 中国 是 从 来的 →

五、看图造句 Make Sentences According to the Pictures

像

____

敢

____

六、回答问题 Answer the Questions

❶ 周爸爸为什么生气？

❷ 周小狄为什么说他要发财了？

七、角色配音 Role Play

两人一组，分别扮演周爸爸和周小狄。

八、中文脱口秀 Chinese Talk Show（1.5 分钟）

你觉得世界上有鬼吗？

文化知识 Cultural Knowledge

中国人对狗的态度

Chinese Attitude towards Dogs

“狗”在中文里也可称作“犬”，中国有悠久的养狗历史，古代中国人养狗主要为了看家、狩猎或作为食物。在中国传统文化中，狗的地位不高，许多与狗有关的词语是贬义词，比如“猪狗不如”“狼心狗肺”等。现代中国人对狗的态度有很大改变，狗已经成为许多家庭里的宠物，甚至被当作家庭成员看待。中国人对狗的态度是复杂的，目前大部分中国人视之为宠物，也有一些人视之为食物（往往与当地的传统风俗有关）。中国不仅有宠物犬，还有很多工作犬。

China has a long history of keeping dogs. People kept dogs mainly for guarding their homes, hunting and as food in ancient Chinese. In traditional Chinese culture, the status of dogs is low so that many words related to dogs are derogatory words, such as “ worse than pigs or dogs” “be as cruel as a wolf ” and so on. Modern Chinese people's attitude towards dogs has changed a lot. Dogs have become pets in many families and are even treated as family members. Attitudes towards dogs in China are mixed, some of Chinese now viewing them as pets, while some view them as food which is often linked to local traditions. There are not only pet dogs in China, but also many working dogs.

第十一课　超级眼镜 The Super Glasses

（电影片段 34：32—38：54）

生词 Words/Phrases

1. 如果	rúguǒ	conj.	if, in case
2. 打败	dǎbài	v.	to defeat
3. 凶恶	xiōng'è	adj.	atrocious, ferocious
4. 证明	zhèngmíng	v.	to prove
5. 太空	tàikōng	n.	outer space
6. 复习	fùxí	v.	to review
7. 帮忙	bāng máng	v.	to help
8. 戴	dài	v.	to wear (accessories)
9. 眼镜	yǎnjìng	n.	glasses, spectacles
10. 受伤	shòu shāng	v.	to be hurt, to be injured
11. 苍蝇	cāngying	n.	fly
12. 成绩	chéngjì	n.	grade, achievement
13. 检查	jiǎnchá	v.	to check, to examine

语法点 Grammar Notes

1 “如果……（的话），（主语）就……”

“如果”后边的分句是一个假设，“就”后边的分句是在这种假设情况下产生的结果。第二个分句的主语要放在“就”前边。

The clause following “如果” is a hypothesis, and the clause after “就” is the result based on the hypothesis. The subject of the second clause should be put before “就”.

例如 Example

（1）**如果**你生病了，**就**去看医生。

（2）**如果**你看到红绿灯，**就**往右走。

（3）**如果**你考试考得好（**的话**），我**就**给你买新电脑。

（4）**如果**你能打败这个地球上最凶恶的狗，那**就**证明你真的是太空超人狗。（电影原句）

2 "第"表示顺序

"第"常放在数量短语前边表示顺序。

"第" is often used before a numeral-measure phrase to indicate order.

例如 Example

（1）**第**一个朋友

（2）**第**二只小猫

（3）**第**三次游泳

（4）周小狄**第**一次拿一百分。（电影原句）

3 动量补语"次"

"次"常放在谓语动词的后边表示动作发生、进行的次数。宾语是地点名词时，动量补语可以放在宾语前，也可以放在宾语后；宾语是人称代词时，动量补语要放在宾语后。

The complement of frequency "次" is usually used after a predicate verb, indicating the number of times that an action has taken place. When the object of the verb is a place, the complement of frequency can be put either before or after the object, however, when the object of the verb is a personal pronoun, the complement of frequency should be put after the object.

例如 Example

（1）我坐过五**次**飞机。

（2）他去过中国三**次**。/他去过三**次**中国。

（3）他问过我很多**次**。

（4）周小狄第一**次**拿一百分。（电影原句）

综合练习 Comprehensive Exercises

一、选择恰当的词语填空并朗读 Choose the Proper Words to Fill in the Blanks and Read the Sentences Aloud

成绩　戴　受伤　如果　打败

1. ________没有水，鱼就不能生存。
2. 他永远不会被________。
3. 外面下雪了，最好________手套。
4. 姐姐打排球时________了。
5. 我的学习________比去年提高了。

二、听后重复句子 Repeat after Listening

三、判断对错 Ture or False

1. 长江七号比那条狗厉害。（　）
2. 周小狄取得了好成绩，因为他好好复习了。（　）
3. 曹主任的眼镜被蛋挞头和小芬打破了。（　）
4. 周小狄以前考过一百分。（　）

四、连词成句 Rearrange the Words or Phrases to Make Sentences

1. 是　他　男朋友　我的　第二个 →
2. 那个　来过　商店　她　几次 →
3. 公司　我　证明　能　他　在 →
4. 忙　你　谢谢　帮　我 →

五、看图造句 Make Sentences According to the Pictures

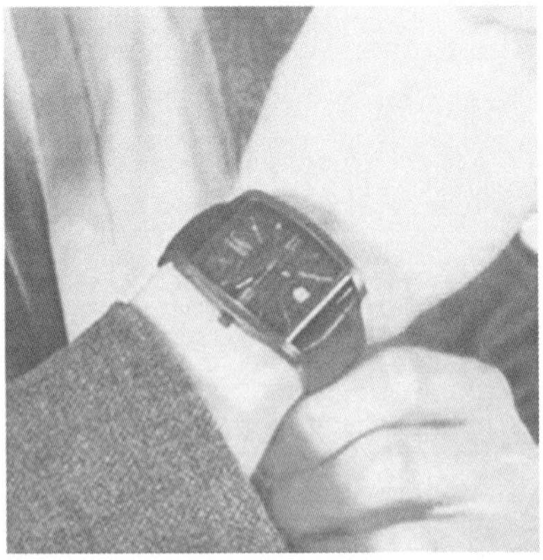

戴

检查

______________________ ______________________

六、回答问题 Answer the Questions

❶ 长江七号是怎么帮助周小狄拿一百分的？

❷ 曹主任为什么要检查周小狄的眼镜？

七、角色配音 Role Play

两人一组，分别扮演周小狄和曹主任。

八、中文脱口秀 Chinese Talk Show（2 分钟）

如果你有超级眼镜，你会用它来做什么？

文化知识 Cultural Knowledge

功夫巨星：李小龙
Kung Fu Superstar：Li Xiaolong/Bruce Lee

李小龙，1940 年出生于美国加利福尼亚州旧金山市，祖籍为中国广东省佛山市。李小龙是世界著名武术家、截拳道创始人、中国功夫首位全球推广者，他革命性地推动了世界武术和功夫电影的发展。他的代表电影作品有《唐山大兄》《精武门》《猛龙过江》等，他在全球拥有大量影迷，是知名度最高的华人之一，也是很多人的精神偶像。1973 年，李小龙在香港拍摄电影时突然去世，但他自强不息、永不言败的精神却一直不分时代、国界地影响着后世。

Li Xiaolong/Bruce Lee, was born in 1940 in San Francisco, California. His ancestral hometown is Foshan, Guangdong Province, China. Li Xiaolong is the world-famous martial artist, founder of the Jeet Kune Do, the first global promoter of kung fu, revolutionary in promoting the development of the world martial arts and kung fu movie. His famous film works includes *The Big Boss*, *Fists of Fury*, *The Way of the Dragon*, etc. With a lot of fans in the whole world, Li Xiaolong is one of the most famous Chinese and also the spirit idol of a lot of people. Li Xiaolong died suddenly while filming a movie in Hong Kong in 1973. But his unyielding, never-ending spirit has continued to influence generations regardless of age and national boundaries.

第十二课　超级运动鞋 The Super Sneakers

（电影片段 38：55—43：38）

生词 Words/Phrases

1. 果然	guǒrán	adv.	as expected，really
2. 天分	tiānfèn	n.	talent，genius
3. 腰	yāo	n.	waist
4. 合	hé	v.	to unite，to combine
5. 充足	chōngzú	adj.	ample，sufficient
6. 睡眠	shuìmián	n.	sleep
7. 创	chuàng	v.	to create，to produce
8. 纪录	jìlù	n. /v.	record，note；to record，to note down
9. 需要	xūyào	v.	to need
10. 合情理	hé qínglǐ	phr.	within reason
11. 过分	guòfèn	adj.	excessive
12. 疯	fēng	adj.	crazy，mad
13. 抓	zhuā	v.	to grab，to seize
14. 冷静	lěngjìng	adj.	calm，composed
15. 难度	nándù	n.	difficulty
16. 叫	jiào	v.	to let
17. 过头	guòtóu	adj.	excessive，undue
18. 梦	mèng	n.	dream

语法点 Grammar Notes

1 “（就/快）要……了”

“（就/快）要……了”表示某事将要发生。如果句中有时间状语，只能用“（就）要……了”。

The structure “（就/快）要……了” indicates that something is going to happen. If there is an adverbial of time in the sentence, then only “（就）要……了” can be used.

例如 Example

（1）**（就/快）要**下雨**了**，你有伞吗？

（2）新年**（就/快）要**到**了**，还有一周。

（3）八点**（就）要**上课**了**，快起床吧。

（4）马上**要**上体育课**了**，我要一双超级运动鞋！（电影原句）

2 兼语句

兼语句的谓语是由两个动词短语组成，前一个动词的宾语是第二个动词的主语，前一个动词经常是“请”“让”“叫”等词语。另外，“使”“让”“叫”后搭配兼语可以表示致使的意思，“使”常用于书面语，“叫”“让”常用于口语。

The predicate of a pivotal sentence is made up of two verbal phrases, the object of the first verb being the subject of the second. The first verb is often a causative verb, such as “请”“让”“叫”. Besides, “使”“让”“叫” can all be followed by a pivotal element to mean “to cause”, “使” usually used in written Chinese, while “叫”“让” usually used in spoken Chinese.

例如 Example

（1）晚上我**请**你们吃饭。

（2）外面有人敲门，我**让/叫**他去看看。

（3）运动**使**人快乐。

（4）我给妈妈买了一件衣服，想**让/叫**她高兴高兴。

（5）**叫**你自己要乖的嘛，每次都睡过头。（电影原句）

综合练习 Comprehensive Exercises

一、选择恰当的词语填空并朗读 Choose the Proper Words to Fill in the Blanks and Read the Sentences Aloud

冷静　需要　果然　梦　过分

1. ________是她得了第一名。
2. 我________两张飞机票。
3. 做人和做事都不能太________。
4. 他是一个________、自信的人。
5. 妻子每天晚上都会做________。

二、听后重复句子 Repeat after Listening

三、判断对错 Ture or False

1. 体育老师比周小狄跳得高。 (　　)
2. 超级运动鞋可以用来跳高、跑步、游泳、踢足球。 (　　)
3. 今天周小狄起床没起晚。 (　　)
4. 其实周小狄昨晚在做梦。 (　　)

四、连词成句 Rearrange the Words or Phrases to Make Sentences

1. 马上　电影　了　就要　开始 →
2. 老师　我　让　想想　再 →
3. 他的　打破　纪录　被　了 →
4. 一点儿　请　冷静　你 →

五、看图造句 Make Sentences According to the Pictures

抓

____

难度

____

六、回答问题 Answer the Questions

❶ 周小狄为什么跳得那么高、游得那么快？

❷ 周小狄为什么觉得他考试能拿一百分？

七、角色配音 Role Play

三人一组，分别扮演周小狄、体育老师和周爸爸。

八、中文脱口秀 Chinese Talk Show（2 分钟）

最近你做过什么有意思的梦？

文化知识 Cultural Knowledge

中国的体育明星
Chinese Sports Stars

除了乒乓球运动明星之外，中国还有很多体育明星，比如排球运动员郎平，她多次帮助中国女排获得世界冠军，被称为“铁榔头”；体操运动员李宁，他曾在单次奥运会上获得三块金牌，被称为“体操王子”，并创办了自己的体育用品公司；篮球运动员姚明，他身高2.26米，被称为“小巨人”，入选奈史密斯篮球名人纪念堂；田径运动员刘翔，被称为“亚洲飞人”，多次获得110米跨栏世界冠军。

In addition to table tennis stars, China also has many sports stars, such as Lang Ping, a volleyball player known as the “Iron Hammer”, who helped the Chinese women's volleyball team win world championships many times. Gymnast Li Ning, who won three gold medals in a single Olympics and was known as the “prince of gymnastics”, founded his own sporting goods company. Basketball player Yao Ming, 2.26 meters tall, known as the “little giant”, was elected to the Naismith Memorial Basketball Hall of Fame. Track and field athlete Liu Xiang, known as the “Flying Man of Asia”, is a multiple 110 m hurdles world champion.

汉语成语 Chinese Idiom

“苦海无涯，回头是岸”意为“人生就像无边的苦海，回头才能看到岸”。比喻只有悔过才能得到解脱。

“苦海无涯，回头是岸” literally means “boundless is the sea of bitterness, turn your head to see the shore”, used metaphorically to indicate that the repentance is salvation.

第十三课　失望的周小狄 Disappointed Zhou Xiaodi

（电影片段 43：39—50：05）

生词 Words/Phrases

1. 装	zhuāng	v.	to pretend；to load
2. 傻	shǎ	adj.	stupid，foolish
3. 玩笑	wánxiào	n.	joke
4. 法宝	fǎbǎo	n.	magic weapon
5. 认真	rènzhēn	adj.	serious，earnest
6. 坨	tuó	m.	lump
7. 试	shì	v.	to try
8. 拼	pīn	v.	to put up a desperate fight
9. 最后	zuìhòu	adj. /n.	last；the last one
10. 机会	jīhuì	n.	opportunity
11. 品味	pǐnwèi	n. /v.	taste；to taste
12. 境界	jìngjiè	n.	extent，degree
13. 仔	zǎi	n.	(of domestic animals) young
14. 生气	shēng qì	v.	to get angry
15. 随	suí	v.	to follow，along with
16. 风	fēng	n.	wind
17. 而	ér	conj.	and；furthermore；while
18. 疼	téng	v. /adj.	to love dearly；hurt，painful
19. 捅	tǒng	v.	to stab
20. 科技	kējì	n.	science and technology
21. 趣味	qùwèi	n.	interest，delight
22. 冤枉	yuānwang	v.	to treat unjustly

23. 活该	huógāi	adj.	deserving
24. 差劲	chàjìn	adj.	disappointing, bad
25. 应该	yīnggāi	v.	should
26. 坦白	tǎnbái	v.	to confess
27. 以为	yǐwéi	v.	to think, to believe
28. 难道	nándào	adv.	used in a rhetorical question for emphasis
29. 误会	wùhuì	v. /n.	to misunderstand; misunderstanding

语法点 Grammar Notes

1 “不是……吗”

“不是……吗”常用来表示提醒或者表达说话人的不理解、不满等。

“不是……吗” is often used to remind someone of something or to show confusion or dissatisfaction.

例如 Example

(1) 他要去上课？今天**不是**星期日**吗**？

(2) 你**不是**困了**吗**？怎么不睡觉？

(3) 你**不是**大学生**吗**？这道小学生的题都不会做？

(4) 你**不是**太空超人狗**吗**？(电影原句)

2 “别/不要……了”

祈使句“别/不要……了”表示劝阻或禁止做某件事情。

The imperative sentence “别/不要……了” is used to dissuade or forbid somebody from doing something.

例如 Example

(1) **别/不要**吃**了**，吃太多对身体不好。

(2) **别/不要**玩电脑游戏**了**。

(3) **别/不要**再喝咖啡**了**，你会睡不着觉的。

(4) **别**玩**了**，我是很认真的！(电影原句)

3 疑问代词“怎么”

“怎么＋动词/形容词”用于询问事情的原因，常表示奇怪、惊讶的语气。

The structure "怎么+v. /adj" is used to ask about the reason for something, indicating surprise or astonishment.

例如 Example

(1) 不是说一起去看电影吗，他**怎么**没去？

(2) 一万块？你**怎么**带着这么多钱？

(3) 姐姐**怎么**不高兴？

(4) 我**怎么**会生你气呢？我们是好朋友嘛。(电影原句)

综合练习 Comprehensive Exercises

一、选择恰当的词语填空并朗读 Choose the Proper Words to Fill in the Blanks and Read the Sentences Aloud

疼　活该　生气　认真　冤枉

1. 上课时应该________听讲。
2. 经常________对身体不好。
3. 奶奶一直很________我。
4. 钱不是他偷的，他被________了。
5. 刚才他吃了五个冰棍儿，________拉肚子。

二、听后重复句子 Repeat after Listening

三、判断对错 Ture or False

1. 那条狗把七仔打败了。　(　　)
2. 七仔没给周小狄法宝。　(　　)
3. 周小狄这次考试得了一百分。　(　　)
4. 最后周小狄知道自己做错了。　(　　)

四、连词成句 Rearrange the Words or Phrases to Make Sentences

❶ 了 他 别 打电话 给→

❷ 累 今天 怎么 你 这么→

❸ 不 难道 上课 明天→

❹ 误会 可能 我们 他 了→

五、看图造句 Make Sentences According to the Pictures

应该

以为

六、回答问题 Answer the Questions

❶ 七仔没有法宝，周小狄是怎么对七仔的？

❷ 为什么周小狄觉得自己做错了？

七、中文脱口秀 Chinese Talk Show（2分钟）

你有没有误会过别人？后来怎么样了？

文化知识 Cultural Knowledge

中国的考试制度

The Examination System in China

中国的高考被认为是最重要、影响力最大的考试，它的全称是“普通高等学校招生全国统一考试”，参加考试的对象一般是全日制普通高中毕业生。高考是科举制度的继承和发展，一般认为科举制度起源于隋朝，结束于清朝末期，历经 1300 多年，并深刻地影响了东亚各国。高考最早开始于 1952 年，现在一般在每年 6 月上旬举行，2021 年中国高考总人数超过 1078 万人。

Gaokao is considered the most important and influential test in China. It stands for the National College Entrance Examination which generally administered to full-time high school graduates. The National College Entrance Examination is the inheritance and development of the imperial examination system, which is believed to have originated in the Sui Dynasty and ended in the late Qing Dynasty. The imperial examination, which has lasted for more than 1,300 years, has had a profound influence on east Asian countries. The exam, which was first held in 1952 and is now held in early June every year. There were more than 10. 78 million participants in 2021.

汉语成语 Chinese Idiom

“小菜一碟” 比喻小事一桩，很容易就能办成。

“小菜一碟” means “a piece of cake”, in the metaphorical sense it indicates something is easy to do.

例如 Example

四百米游泳对他来说是小菜一碟。

第十四课　重逢 Meet Again

（电影片段 50：06—54：49）

生词 Words/Phrases

1. 以后	yǐhòu	n.	after，hereafter
2. 原来	yuánlái	adv. /adj.	so that is how it is；original
3. 眨	zhǎ	v.	to blink，to wink
4. 借	jiè	v.	to borrow，to lend
5. 盖子	gàizi	n.	lid，cover
6. 充	chōng	v.	to fill
7. 弹力	tánlì	n.	elasticity
8. 还原	huán yuán	v.	to restore to the original state or shape
9. 够	gòu	v.	to be enough
10. 说谎	shuō huǎng	v.	to lie
11. 人才	réncái	n.	talented person，person with ability
12. 缘故	yuángù	n.	cause，reason
13. 幸运	xìngyùn	adj.	lucky，fortunate
14. 盒	hé	n.	box，case

语法点 Grammar Notes

1 “呢”询问处所

“名词＋呢”可以用来询问人或事物在哪儿。

“n. ＋呢” is used to ask about where somebody or something is.

例如 Example

（1）你的车**呢**？

（2）钱包**呢**？你看见了吗？

（3）红色的杯子**呢**？怎么不见了？

（4）它的盖子**呢**？从哪里充电？（电影原句）

2 动词结构做定语

动词或动词短语做定语时，定语和中心语之间要加“的”。

When a verb or verb phrase is used as an attributive modifier, “的” should be put between the modifier and the word modified.

例如 Example

（1）他做**的**饭

（2）新买**的**电视

（3）上过大学**的**人

（4）我们这些没读过书**的**人（电影原句）

3 助词“的”“地”“得”

“的”一般用在定语和定语所修饰的名词之间；“地”用在状语和状语所修饰的动词之间；“得”用在动词或形容词后，连接结果补语或程度补语等。

Among the three particles, “的” can be put between an attribute and the noun it modifies, “地” is used to connect an adverbial modifier and the verb it modifies, while “得” is used after a verb or an adjective to introduce a complement of result or degree, etc.

例如 Example

（1）白色**的**床

（2）高兴**地**说

（3）睡**得**早

（4）最热的这天它无缘无故**地**又会动了。（电影原句）

综合练习 Comprehensive Exercises

一、选择恰当的词语填空并朗读 Choose the Proper Words to Fill in the Blanks and Read the Sentences Aloud

幸运　以后　人才　够　原来

1. 再见！________我们还会见面的！
2. ________他姓刘，不姓张。
3. 买十个鸡蛋就________了。
4. 他是体育方面的________。
5. 我找到了一份很好的工作，真________。

二、听后重复句子 Repeat after Listening

三、判断对错 Ture or False

1. 七仔自己回到了周小狄的家。　（　）
2. 周爸爸以前见过七仔这样的"玩具"。　（　）
3. 周爸爸相信七仔是那个球变的。　（　）
4. 七仔把电风扇修好了。　（　）

四、连词成句 Rearrange the Words or Phrases to Make Sentences

4 一起　的人　和你　吃饭　是谁 →

5 去年　这是　的　电影 →

5 他　北京大学　地　幸运　上了 →

5 慢　她　得　跑　很 →

五、看图造句 Make Sentences According to the Pictures

借

____

充

____

六、回答问题 Answer the Questions

❹ 周爸爸为什么觉得七仔是高科技玩具？

❺ 周爸爸和周小狄那天睡得怎么样？

七、角色配音 Role Play

两人一组，分别扮演周爸爸和周小狄。

八、中文脱口秀 Chinese Talk Show（2 分钟）

七仔会什么“魔法”？

提示：“把”字句。

文化知识 Cultural Knowledge

华语电影五大奖
The Five Chinese Film Awards

华语电影五大奖是华语影坛影响力最大的五个奖项，分别是金鸡奖、百花奖、华表奖、金像奖和金马奖。金鸡奖（设立于 1981 年）是中国内地最权威和最专业的电影奖，当年属中国农历鸡年，因此得名，百花奖（设立于 1962 年）由观众投票产生，是中国历史最悠久的电影奖，华表奖（设立于 1994 年）由中国政府颁发，金像奖（设立于 1982 年）和金马奖（设立于 1962 年）分别是香港、台湾地区最重要的电影奖项。

The five Chinese film awards are the five most influential awards in the Chinese film industry, namely the Golden Rooster Awards, the Hundred Flowers Awards, the Huabiao Film Awards, Hong Kong Film Awards and the Golden Horse Awards. The Golden Rooster Awards (established in 1981) is the most authoritative and professional film award in interior China. It was established in the year of the rooster in the Chinese lunar calendar, hence the Golden Rooster Awards. The Hundred Flowers Awards (established in 1962) is voted by the audience and is the oldest film award in China. The Huabiao Awards (established in 1994) is awarded by the Chinese government. Hong Kong Film Awards (established in 1982) and the Golden Horse Awards (established in 1962) are the most important film awards in Hong Kong and Taiwan respectively.

第十五课　又打架了 Another Fight

（电影片段 54：50—59：00）

生词 Words/Phrases

1. 包	bāo	n.	bag，sack
2. 拉	lā	v.	to pull，to drag
3. 追	zhuī	v.	to chase，to go after
4. 工具	gōngjù	n.	tool，instrument
5. 箱	xiāng	n.	box，bin
6. 直接	zhíjiē	adj.	direct，straight
7. 锯	jù	v. /n.	to saw；saw

语法点 Grammar Notes

1 语气助词“啊”

语气助词“啊”用在句末，可使句子带上一层感情色彩。“啊”常受到前一字尾音的影响而发生不同的变音，书写时可按变音写成不同的字。

The modal particle “啊” is used at the end of a sentence to set the mood. The pronunciation of “啊” varies with the finals of the syllables before it，and in written Chinese，the variants are represented by different characters sometimes.

the final of the syllable before 啊	the pronunciation of 啊
a，o，e，i，ü	ya（呀）
u，ao，ou，uo，iu	ua（哇）
n	na（哪）
zhi，chi，shi，ri	ra

例如 Example

（1）你书包里面是什么东西**啊**（→呀）？（电影原句）

（2）他在哪里住**啊**（→哇）？

（3）这道题很简单**啊**（→哪）。

（4）大家吃**啊**（→ra）。

2 语气助词“吧”

语气助词“吧”用在祈使句末尾，表示建议或者命令别人，可使语气缓和。

When used at the end of an imperative sentence, the modal particle “吧” indicates a suggestion or command with a softened mood.

例如 Example

（1）说**吧**。

（2）今天我没时间，你明天来**吧**。

（3）家里的桌子坏了，再买一张**吧**。

（4）直接来**吧**。（电影原句）

综合练习 Comprehensive Exercises

一、选择恰当的词语填空并朗读 Choose the Proper Words to Fill in the Blanks and Read the Sentences Aloud

包　箱　拉　直接　追

1. 妈妈的________丢了。
2. 开门要往里________，不是往外推。
3. 哥哥跑得太快，我________不上。
4. 请把纸扔到垃圾________里。
5. 下课后我们________去火车站。

二、听后重复句子 Repeat after Listening

三、判断对错 Ture or False

❶ 今天七仔很有精神。 （ ）

❷ 蛋挞头抓住了七仔。 （ ）

❸ 他们把七仔锯开了。 （ ）

❹ 美娇不想打架。 （ ）

四、连词成句 Rearrange the Words or Phrases to Make Sentences

❶ 一点儿 你 再吃 吧 水果 →

❷ 他 晚上 没 昨天 睡好 →

❸ 行李箱 过来 请 拉 把 →

❹ 钱包 钱 没有 我的 里面 →

五、看图造句 Make Sentences According to the Pictures

追

____

锯

____

六、回答问题 Answer the Questions

❶ 七仔使用“魔法”修好电扇后会怎么样？

❷ 美娇为什么要保护周小狄？

七、角色配音 Role Play

四人一组，分别扮演周小狄、蛋挞头、暴龙和美娇。

八、中文脱口秀 Chinese Talk Show（2 分钟）

请谈谈学生之间的欺凌问题。

提示：暴力、伤害、言语、网络、保护等。

文化知识 Cultural Knowledge

动画电影《长江七号爱地球》
Animated Film *CJ7*：*The Cartoon*

《长江七号爱地球》于 2010 年在中国上映，是一部面向儿童的动画电影。这部作品的人物和故事背景与原作《长江七号》基本相同，电影后半部分加入了“环境保护”的主题：袁老师带着全班同学去春游，但原本山清水秀的“美丽谷”已经被严重污染，在更大的环境灾难即将发生之际，七仔挺身而出，用尽自己的能量拯救了地球。这部电影中有很多向经典电影致敬的画面。

CJ7：*The Cartoon* was released in China in 2010 as an animated film aimed at children. The characters and story background are same with the original *CJ7*, but joined the theme of “environmental protection” at the second half of the movie. Miss Yuan takes the classmates to go spring outing, but otherwise picturesque scenery “beautiful valley” has been seriously polluted. While the larger environment disaster is happening, CJ7 stands out and use its own energy to save the earth. The film has many scenes to pay homage to classic movies.

汉语成语 Chinese Idiom

“没（无）精打采”意为“不高兴，不振作”。

“没（无）精打采” means to be unhappy or in low spirits.

例如 Example

他昨天睡得很晚，今天上课没（无）精打采的。

第十六课　我们是朋友 We are Friends

（电影片段 59：01—60：51）

生词 Words/Phrases

1. 全	quán	adj.	all，whole
2. 到底	dàodǐ	adv.	(used in question for emphasis) on earth
3. 聪明	cōngmíng	adj.	clever，smart
4. 干	gàn	v.	to do，to act
5. 伤心	shāng xīn	adj.	sad，sorrowful
6. 着火	zháo huǒ	v.	to catch fire
7. 中	zhòng	v.	to win (in a lottery)
8. 彩票	cǎipiào	n.	lottery ticket
9. 光	guāng	adj. /n.	nothing left，all gone；light
10. 烟花	yānhuā	n.	firework
11. 秘密	mìmì	n. /adj.	secret
12. 当然	dāngrán	adv.	of course
13. 蛮	mán	adv.	very，quite
14. 加入	jiārù	v.	to join，to accede
15. 柔道	róudào	n.	judo，jiujitsu
16. 队	duì	n.	team

语法点 Grammar Notes

1 副词“到底”

副词“到底”用在疑问句或者带疑问代词的非疑问句中，表示进一步探究，不能用于带“吗”的是非疑问句中；如果句子主语是疑问代词，“到底”只能放在主语前。动词“到底”表示到尽头、到终点。

The adverb“到底”is used in an interrogative sentence or a sentence with an interrogative pronoun, indicating to probe further. It cannot be used in a yes-no question with“吗”.“到底”should be put before the subject if the subject is the interrogative pronoun. The verb“到底”means“till the end”.

例如 Example

(1) 你刚才说去公园，现在又说去商场，你**到底**要去哪里？

(2) 她说是她做的，你说是你做的，**到底**是谁做的？

(3) 虽然他已经二十岁了，但说**到底**他还只是一个孩子。

(4) 这**到底**是什么呀？（电影原句）

2 动词“中”

动词“中”意思是正对上、恰好合上，也可以表示受到、遭受。

The verb“中”means“to match”, but can also mean“to suffer”.

例如 Example

(1) 他看**中**了那辆蓝色的车。

(2) 今天太热，小心**中**暑。

(3) **中**了彩票！（电影原句）

3 语气助词“呢”

语气助词“呢”用于陈述句句尾，或用在形容词谓语句和动词谓语句后边，表示确认事实，使对方信服，含有夸张的语气。

The modal particle“呢”can be used at the end of a declarative sentence or after a sentence with an adjectival or verbal predicate to confirm a fact and convince someone in an exaggerative mood.

例如 Example

(1) 别着急，现在时间还早**呢**。

(2) 他那么忙，才不会来**呢**。

(3) 小孩子的事情，才不告诉大人**呢**。（电影原句）

综合练习 Comprehensive Exercises

一、选择恰当的词语填空并朗读 Choose the Proper Words to Fill in the Blanks and Read the Sentences Aloud

当然　全　秘密　干　加入

❶ ________班都认识了这位新同学。

❷ 那件事不是她________的。

❸ 我不会把这个________告诉别人。

❹ 我们________是朋友。

❺ 他想________学校的篮球队。

二、听后重复句子 Repeat after Listening

三、判断对错 Ture or False

❶ 七仔跑回来了。（　）

❷ 周小狄告诉同学们哪里可以买到七仔。（　）

❸ 蛋挞头把七仔的事告诉曹主任了。（　）

❹ 美娇不会再被同学们嘲笑了。（　）

四、连词成句 Rearrange the Words or Phrases to Make Sentences

❶ 那个　打中　我　球　没有 →

❷ 怎么　到底　这个　汉字　写 →

❸ 他　孩子　还是　呢　小 →

❹ 妹妹　了　吃光　被　巧克力 →

五、看图造句 Make Sentences According to the Pictures

伤心

____

着火

____

六、回答问题 Answer the Questions

❶ 七仔会做什么表情？

❷ 周小狄和同学们以后还会打架吗？

七、角色配音 Role Play

几人一组，分别扮演周小狄、蛋挞头和其他同学。

八、中文脱口秀 Chinese Talk Show（2 分钟）

小时候你有什么没有告诉大人的秘密？

提示：……的时候。

文化知识 Cultural Knowledge

普　通　话
Mandarin

中国推行的国家通用语言文字包括普通话和规范汉字。普通话是以北京语音为标准音、以北方官话为基础方言、以典范的现代白话文著作为语法规范的现代标准汉语，也是中外文化交流的重要工具和外国人学习汉语的首选语言。推广普通话是为了消除语言隔阂，协助社会交际，与人们使用和传承方言并不矛盾。教育部等部门提出，到 2025 年，全国范围内普通话普及率应达到 85%。

The national common language in China includes Mandarin and standardized Chinese characters. Mandarin is a modern standard Chinese with Beijing pronunciation as the standard pronunciation, Mandarin in northern China as the basic dialect, and typical modern vernacular writings as the grammatical norm. It is also an important tool for cultural exchanges between China and foreign countries and the first choice for foreigners to learn Chinese. The purpose of popularizing Mandarin is to eliminate language barriers and assist social communication, which is not contradictory to the people's use and inheritance of dialects. The Ministry of Education and other departments have proposed that by 2025, the nationwide Mandarin popularization rate should reach 85%.

汉语成语 Chinese Idiom

"一言为定"意为"一句话说定了，不再改变"，经常单独使用。

"一言为定" means "it is a deal/promise", usually used independently.

例如 Example

A：明年我们去国外旅游怎么样？

B：好，一言为定。

第十七课　一百分还是零分 One Hundred or Zero

（电影片段 60：52—62：09）

生词 Words/Phrases

1. 了不起	liǎobuqǐ	adj.	great, amazing
2. 滚	gǔn	v.	to get out; to roll
3. 作弊	zuò bì	v.	to cheat
4. 贱	jiàn	adj.	cheap, lowly
5. 骨头	gǔtou	n.	bone
6. 胡说	húshuō	v.	to talk nonsense
7. 墨水	mòshuǐ	n.	ink
8. 一样	yīyàng	adj.	same, as…as…
9. 明明	míngmíng	adv.	obviously, undoubtedly
10. 改	gǎi	v.	to change, to modify
11. 久	jiǔ	adj.	for a long time, long
12. 准	zhǔn	v. /adj.	to allow, to permit; exact, precise

语法点 Grammar Notes

1 副词"才"

副词"才"可以表示只有在某种条件下才产生某种结果，前面通常有"只有""必须"或含有此类意思的词。"才"也可以表示强调，句尾常用"呢"。

The adverb "才" indicates a certain result or conclusion can be produced only under certain conditions, usually preceded by "只有" "必须" or words with such meanings. "才" can also express a emphatic tone, usually with "呢" in the end of sentence.

例如 Example

（1）只有努力**才**能有好成绩。

（2）他有时间**才**去运动。

（3）这是秘密，我**才**不会告诉他呢。

（4）他作弊**才**考到六十分。（电影原句）

2 副词“明明”

副词“明明”多用于口语，表示很明显、情况就是这样。用“明明”的小句前后常有反问或表示转折的小句。

The adverb “明明” is often used in spoken Chinese, indicates a obvious situation or fact. A rhetorical question or turning sentence can be put before or after the sentence with “明明”.

例如 Example

（1）门铃响了，但外面**明明**没有人。

（2）这本书**明明**是我的，不是他的。

（3）我**明明**把水放在桌子上了，怎么不见了？

（4）**明明**是零分，自己改成一百分的。（电影原句）

综合练习 Comprehensive Exercises

一、选择恰当的词语填空并朗读 Choose the Proper Words to Fill in the Blanks and Read the Sentences Aloud

久　准　一样　胡说　明明

1. 别听他________，他在骗人。
2. 我的笔和别人的不________。
3. 那个人________是开车来的。
4. 你多________没运动了？
5. 上课时不________吃东西。

二、听后重复句子 Repeat after Listening

三、判断对错 Ture or False

❶ 周小狄真的考了一百分。 （ ）

❷ 周爸爸不相信周小狄考试作弊。 （ ）

❸ 其实周小狄考了零分。 （ ）

❹ 老板不让周爸爸上班了。 （ ）

四、连词成句 Rearrange the Words or Phrases to Make Sentences

❶ 明明 错 这个字 的 是 →

❷ 会 多运动 才 好 身体 →

❸ 不 这 衣服 两件 一样 →

❹ 手机 不准 考试 时 用 →

五、看图造句 Make Sentences According to the Pictures

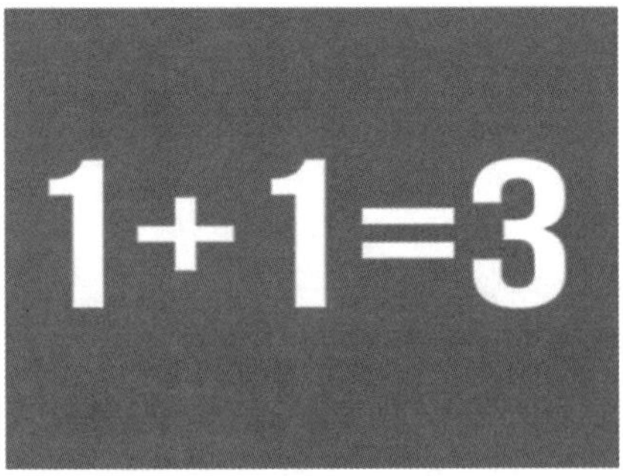

了不起

改

____

____

六、回答问题 Answer the Questions

❶ 老板为什么不相信周小狄能考一百分？

❷ 周爸爸应该打老板吗？为什么？

七、角色配音 Role Play

两人一组，分别扮演周爸爸和老板。

八、中文脱口秀 Chinese Talk Show（2 分钟）

你对学生考试作弊有什么看法？

提示：欺骗、诚实、诚信等。

文化知识 Cultural Knowledge

中国电影知识
About Chinese Films

中国有许多经典电影，例如《一江春水向东流》《地道战》《芙蓉镇》《活着》《大红灯笼高高挂》《黄土地》《阳光灿烂的日子》等。中国电影也获得过许多国际奖项，例如张艺谋导演的《红高粱》曾获得柏林国际电影节金熊奖，陈凯歌导演的《霸王别姬》曾获得戛纳电影节金棕榈奖，贾樟柯导演的《三峡好人》曾获得威尼斯国际电影节金狮奖。

There are many classic movies in China, such as *Spring River Flows East*, *Tunnel Warfare*, *Hibiscus Town*, *To Live*, *Raise the Red Lantern*, *Yellow Earth*, *In the Heat of the Sun* and so on. Chinese films have also won many international awards. For example, *Red Sorghum* directed by Zhang Yimou won the Golden Bear at the Berlin International Film Festival. *Farewell My Concubine* directed by Chen Kaige won The Golden Palm at the Cannes Film Festival. *Still Life* directed by Jia Zhangke has won the Golden Lion at the Venice International Film Festival.

第十八课　生气的周爸爸 Angry Dad

（电影片段 62：10—64：38）

生词 Words/Phrases

1. 老实	lǎoshi	adj.	honest，frank
2. 鸭蛋	yādàn	n.	duck egg
3. 结果	jiéguǒ	n.	result
4. 自己	zìjǐ	pron.	self
5. 搞	gǎo	v.	(followed by a complement) to produce a certain effect or result
6. 辛苦	xīnkǔ	adj.	hard，toilsome
7. 烦	fán	adj.	vexed，annoyed
8. 反正	fǎnzhèng	adv.	anyway，no matter what
9. 种	zhǒng	m.	kind，type
10. 总是	zǒngshì	adv.	always
11. 管	guǎn	v.	to manage，to administer
12. 能耐	néngnai	n.	ability，capability
13. 本事	běnshi	n.	ability，capability
14. 赖皮	làipí	v.	to renegue
15. 嘴（巴）	zuǐ（ba）	n.	mouth
16. 嚣张	xiāozhāng	adj.	arrogant，rampant

语法点 Grammar Notes

1 副词“反正”

副词“反正”表示情况虽然不同但结果并无区别，还可以表示坚决肯定的语气。

The adverb “反正” is used to indicate the same result despite different circumstances, also can express a firm or determined tone.

例如 Example

(1) 他去不去没关系，**反正**我会去。

(2) 你买什么都可以，**反正**他花钱。

(3) 你别再说了，**反正**我不吃。

(4) **反正**都已经改了，你能怎么样？（电影原句）

2 副词“就”

副词“就”后加动词可以表示承接上文，得出结论，或在某种情况下，产生某种结果。

The adverb “就” can be followed by a verb to indicate a conclusion or a resolution made on the basis of what has been mentioned previously, or indicate a certain result can be produced under certain conditions.

例如 Example

(1) 你病了，**就**在家休息吧。

(2) 这儿的茶不错，**就**喝茶吧。

(3) 没驾照**就**不能开车。

(4) 凭什么？**就**凭我是你老爸，行不行？（电影原句）

综合练习 Comprehensive Exercises

一、选择恰当的词语填空并朗读 Choose the Proper Words to Fill in the Blanks and Read the Sentences Aloud

反正　结果　辛苦　赖皮　烦

1. 他喝了很多咖啡，________晚上睡不着了。
2. 你工作做得不错，________了。
3. 别理我，我现在很________。

4 其他人谁去都行，________不能让他去。
5 说话要算话，不能________。

二、听后重复句子 Repeat after Listening

三、判断对错 Ture or False

1 因为怕爸爸不高兴，所以周小狄改了成绩。 (　　)
2 周小狄以后还能和七仔玩。 (　　)
3 周爸爸不想再管周小狄了。 (　　)
4 周小狄要靠自己考六十分。 (　　)

四、连词成句 Rearrange the Words or Phrases to Make Sentences

1 牛奶　这　好喝　种　很 →
2 总是　爸爸　公司　走路　去 →
3 哥哥　本事　自己　很有　觉得 →
4 小　嘴　她　一张　长着 →

五、看图造句 Make Sentences According to the Pictures

搞
____

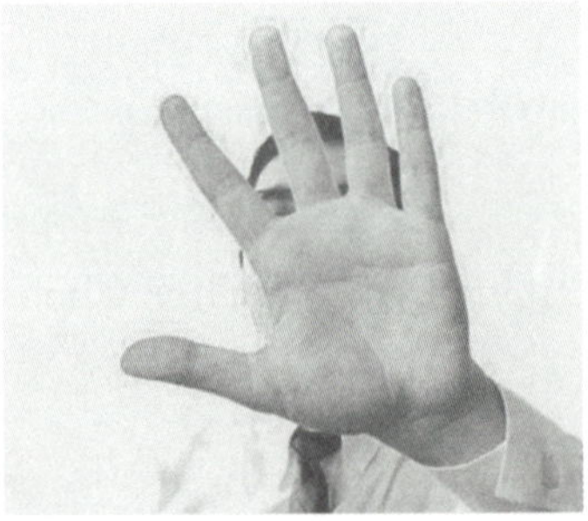

管
____

六、回答问题 Answer the Questions

❶ 周小狄为什么觉得周爸爸好烦？

❷ 周爸爸为什么把七仔拿走了？

七、角色配音 Role Play

两人一组，分别扮演周爸爸和周小狄。

八、中文脱口秀 Chinese Talk Show（2 分钟）

你和父母吵过架吗？为什么吵架？

提示：青春期、叛逆、脾气、理解等。

文化知识 Cultural Knowledge

"（零）鸭蛋"的由来
The Origin of (Zero) Duck Egg

"（零）鸭蛋"通常指在考试或比赛中得了零分，但为什么用"鸭蛋"来表示而不是鸡蛋或鹅蛋呢？有一种说法是，和鹅蛋相比，鸡蛋和鸭蛋更常见，俗语一般会从常见的事物取材。另外，鸭蛋比鸡蛋大，而且鸭子呆头呆脑、走路一摇一摆的样子显得有些笨拙，因此用"（零）鸭蛋"来表示"零分"更形象、更有讽刺效果。

The idiom (zero) duck egg usually refers to a score of zero in an exam or competition, but why use "duck egg" instead of an egg or goose egg? There is a saying that eggs and duck eggs are more common than goose eggs. In addition, duck eggs are bigger than eggs, and the duck looks awkward and clumsy, so it is more vivid and ironic to use (zero) duck egg to mean zero points.

汉语成语 Chinese Idiom

"以大欺小"和"以强凌弱"意义相似，意为"凭借强大去欺负弱小"。

"以大欺小" has a similar meaning to "以强凌弱", means the strong bullies the weak.

例如 Example

他经常以大欺小，同学们都不喜欢他。

第十九课　好心的袁老师 Kind Teacher Yuan

（电影片段 64：39—66：10）

生词 Words/Phrases

1. 忘	wàng	v.	to forget
2. 交	jiāo	v.	to give，to hand in/over
3. 闹别扭	nào bièniu	phr.	be at odds with，be difficult with
4. 介意	jiè yì	v.	to mind
5. 谈	tán	v.	to talk，to discuss
6. 正好	zhènghǎo	adj. /adv.	just in time，just right
7. 温习	wēnxí	v.	to review
8. 功课	gōngkè	n.	schoolwork，homework，lesson
9. 感谢	gǎnxiè	v.	to thank
10. 内疚	nèijiù	adj.	compunctious，guilty
11. 肯	kěn	v.	be willing to
12. 报答	bàodá	v.	to pay back
13. 放心	fàng xīn	v.	to ease one's mind，to rest assured

语法点 Grammar Notes

1 “会”表示可能

助动词“会”在句中表示可能，通常用于未发生的事件。

The auxiliary verb “会” is used in a sentence to indicate a possibility，usually referring to something that hasn't happened.

例如 Example

（1）明天下雪，**会**很冷。

（2）没关系，我不**会**生气的。

（3）你穿得太少了，**会**生病的。

（4）我怕同学**会**笑他。（电影原句）

2 正好

“正好”可以做形容词，表示时间、位置、体积、数量、程度等满足某个条件（不早不晚、不前不后、不大不小、不多不少、不高不低等）。“正好”也可以做副词，表示恰好或遇到某个机会做某事。

“正好” can be used as an adjective to mean “just right”, indicating a certain condition in terms of time, position, size, quantity or degree, etc. is met (it is neither too early nor too late, neither before nor after, neither too big nor too small, neither too much nor too little, neither too high nor too low, etc.). “正好” can also be used as an adverb to mean “it is the right time or opportunity to do something”.

例如 Example

（1）这件衣服**正好**，不大也不小。

（2）你来得**正好**，电影马上就要开始了。

（3）他明天去北京，**正好**我可以和他一起去。

（4）我会和他好好谈一谈，**正好**明天考试也可以帮他温习功课。（电影原句）

3 疑问代词“什么”活用

“什么”可以做指示代词，用来代替不确定的人或事物，表达的语气更客气。有时可以省略“什么”，句子的意思不变。

“什么” can be used as a demonstrative pronoun instead of an indefinite person or thing, making the tone politer. The meaning of the sentence won't change if “什么” is omitted.

例如 Example

（1）这辆车没**什么**问题。

（2）如果有**什么**不懂的地方，可以打电话问我。

（3）今天有没有**什么**高兴的事？

（4）你不用报答我**什么**，这是我应该做的。（电影原句）

综合练习 Comprehensive Exercises

一、选择恰当的词语填空并朗读 Choose the Proper Words to Fill in the Blanks and Read the Sentences Aloud

介意　忘　放心　谈　交

❶ 我永远不会________了她。

❷ 谁还没________作业？

❸ 不要________这种小事情。

❹ 请________一下你对公司的看法。

❺ 女儿一个人在家，我不________。

二、听后重复句子 Repeat after Listening

三、判断对错 Ture or False

❶ 周爸爸进学校给周小狄送饭。（　　）

❷ 周小狄今天会去袁老师家温习功课。（　　）

❸ 袁老师对周小狄非常好。（　　）

❹ 周爸爸知道怎么报答袁老师。（　　）

四、连词成句 Rearrange the Words or Phrases to Make Sentences

❶ 和他　我　会　谈谈　这件事 →

❷ 有没有　电影　最近　什么　好看的 →

❸ 房间　这个　的　正好　温度 →

❹ 感谢　大家　对我　帮助　的 →

五、看图造句 Make Sentences According to the Pictures

内疚

____

报答

____

六、回答问题 Answer the Questions

1. 周爸爸为什么不进学校？
2. 周爸爸为什么很感谢袁老师？

七、角色配音 Role Play

两人一组，分别扮演周爸爸和袁老师。

八、中文脱口秀 Chinese Talk Show（2分钟）

你以后想报答谁？怎么报答？

文化知识 Cultural Knowledge

中国旗袍
Chinese Cheongsam

旗袍是中国甚至世界华人女性的传统服装，是中国服饰文化的代表之一。一般认为旗袍是由清代旗女的服装发展而来，后来又由汉族女性吸收西方服装的样式不断改进而定型，还有观点认为旗袍的起源可以追溯到先秦两汉时期。近年来，旗袍作为中华女性的礼服和“国服”出现在许多重大场合，也在国际时尚舞台上频频亮相。旗袍展现了东方女性的优雅、含蓄、婉约之美，以其独特的魅力而著称。

Cheongsam is a kind of traditional clothing and typical dress of Chinese women in China and even the world, and it is one of the representatives of China apparel culture. It is generally acknowledged that the cheongsam was developed from the clothing of Manchu women in the Qing Dynasty, and was later shaped by Han women absorbing the styles of Western clothing, and there is a third view that the origin of cheongsam can be traced back to the pre-Qin and Han dynasties. In recent years, cheongsam has appeared on many momentous occasions as Chinese women's dresses and "national apparel", and it has also appeared frequently on the international fashion stage. Cheongsam shows the elegant, implicit and graceful beauty of oriental women, and is famous for its unique charm.

第二十课　老板的红包 The Red Envelop from Boss

（电影片段 66：11—68：16）

生词 Words/Phrases

1. 口	kǒu	n./m.	mouth；used for members of families
2. 臭	chòu	adj.	smelly，stinking
3. 同乡	tóngxiāng	n.	a person from the same hometown or province
4. 当面	dāng miàn	adv.	to one's face，in one's presence
5. 收	shōu	v.	to take，to receive
6. 红包	hóngbāo	n.	red envelop，lucky money
7. 要是	yàoshi	conj.	if，supposing
8. 缴	jiǎo	v.	to pay
9. 赶快	gǎnkuài	adv.	hurriedly
10. 开工	kāi gōng	v.	to start working
11. 走运	zǒu yùn	v.	be in luck，be lucky

语法点 Grammar Notes

1 连词“要是”

连词“要是”表示如果、如果是，常用“要是……（的话），就……”结构。“要是”后的句子提出假设，“就”后的句子表示在假设的情况下采取的行动或出现的结果。

The conjunction“要是”means“if，in case”，usually used in the structure“要是……（的话），就……”，in which“要是”introduces a sentence indicating an assumption，and“就”introduces a sentence indicating the action or result consequent upon the assumed situation.

例如 Example

（1）今天**要是**有时间，我就去找你。

（2）**要是**坐车，十分钟就能到。

（3）**要是**那样就谢天谢地了。（电影原句）

2 副词“赶快”

副词“赶快”表示抓紧时间。

The adverb “赶快” means “hurriedly”.

例如 Example

（1）要下雨了，你**赶快**回家吧。

（2）**赶快**穿好衣服，我们马上走。

（3）**赶快**开工！（电影原句）

综合练习 Comprehensive Exercises

一、选择恰当的词语填空并朗读 Choose the Proper Words to Fill in the Blanks and Read the Sentences Aloud

收　口　红包　走运　要是

1. 我的快递到了，我去________一下。
2. 过年了，爷爷奶奶给了我一个大________。
3. 你________太累的话，就休息休息。
4. 他的________水都要流下来了。
5. 今天出去忘了带伞，结果下雨了，真不________。

二、听后重复句子 Repeat after Listening

三、判断对错 Ture or False

❶ 周爸爸又回去工作了。 （ ）

❷ 老板觉得自己当时做得不对。 （ ）

❸ 老板说周小狄将来会成为人才。 （ ）

❹ 老板给周爸爸的钱不多。 （ ）

四、连词成句 Rearrange the Words or Phrases to Make Sentences

❶ 去公园 要是 就 不下雨 我 →

❷ 你 去 起床 赶快 上课 →

❸ 想 我 说几句话 当面 和她 →

❹ 老板 马上 工人 开工 让 →

五、看图造句 Make Sentences According to the Pictures

要是

____

赶快

____

六、回答问题 Answer the Questions

❶ 老板为什么给周爸爸钱？

❷ 周爸爸为什么说自己很走运？

七、角色配音 Role Play

两人一组，分别扮演周爸爸和老板。

八、中文脱口秀 Chinese Talk Show（2 分钟）

你觉得老板这个人怎么样？为什么？

文化知识 Cultural Knowledge

中国的同乡文化
The Townsfolk Culture in China

"同乡"（或"老乡"）指籍贯相同的人。中国人重视乡情，有句俗语是"老乡见老乡，两眼泪汪汪"。"同乡"的使用标准非常宽泛，籍贯地小到一乡，大到一省，都可以称为同乡，甚至籍贯地距离较远但使用同一方言的人，也可以称为同乡或半同乡。以宗亲观念为基础的同乡文化在中国有悠久的历史，在中国古代，同乡文化甚至与政治权力紧密相连。如今，海内外有很多中国人或华人组成的"同乡会"，目的是加强同乡之间的联络、交流、互助。

"Tongxiang" (or "laoxiang") refers to people from the same place of origin. Chinese people value the affection of their hometown. "Tongxiang" is used in a very broad standard, from a small hometown to a large province, can be called tongxiang, or even a distant hometown but the same dialect people can also be called tongxiang or semi-tongxiang. The countryman culture based on the concept of clan has a long history in China. In ancient China, Townsfolk culture was even closely linked with political power. Nowadays, there are many "hometown associations" formed by Chinese people at home and abroad, with the purpose of strengthening contact, communication and mutual assistance between people in their hometown.

汉语成语 Chinese Idioms

"出人头地"意为"超出一般人；高人一等"。

"出人头地" means to succeed, stand out among one's fellows or distinguish oneself.

例如 Example

只有努力学习，才能出人头地。

“谢天谢地”用来形容“感激和庆幸的心情”，可以单独使用。

“谢天谢地” means “thank God/goodness”, often used to express gratitude and thankfulness, can be used independently.

例如 Example

谢天谢地，我终于找到你了。

第二十一课　意外 The Accident

(电影片段 68：17—73：55)

生词 Words/Phrases

1. 及格	jí gé	v.	to pass a exam
2. 安全	ānquán	adj.	safe, secure
3. 带	dài	n.	belt
4. 伸	shēn	v.	to stretch, to extend
5. 搬	bān	v.	to carry, to move
6. 意外	yìwài	n./adj.	accident; unexpected
7. 控制	kòngzhì	v.	to control, to take command of
8. 醒	xǐng	v.	to wake up, to be awake
9. 之后	zhīhòu	n.	after, hereafter

语法点 Grammar Notes

1 名词谓语句

名词谓语句的谓语部分由名词性成分充当，一般用于表达时间、日期、年龄等。

A sentence with a nominal predicate is a sentence whose predicate is a nominal element. It is usually used to indicate time, date, age and so on.

例如 Example

(1) 现在两点半。

(2) 昨天星期六。

(3) 他三十二岁。

2 动词谓语句

动词谓语句的谓语部分由动词性成分充当，有时动词需要加上动态助词、语气词或重叠后才能做谓语。

A sentence with averbal predicate is a sentence whose predicate is a verbal element. Sometimes the verb is followed by aspect particles, modal particles, or use the reduplicative form to make predicates.

例如 Example

（1）你看。

（2）手机响了。

（3）你回去吧。

（4）我想一想。

（5）你出来一下。（电影原句）

3 形容词谓语句

形容词谓语句的结构是"主语＋程度副词＋形容词"，形容词用来描述人或事物的性质或状态，程度副词经常用"很"。否定形式为"主语＋不＋形容词"。

In sentences with an adjectival predicate, the structure is "subject＋adverb of degree＋adjective", the adjective describes the nature or state of somebody or something, usually following the adverb of degree "很". The negative form is "subject＋不＋adjective".

例如 Example

（1）姐姐很漂亮。

（2）这个菜不好吃。

（3）我很累了。（电影原句）

4 主谓谓语句

主谓谓语句中的结构是"全句主语＋全句谓语（主语＋谓语）"，全句谓语中的主语常常是全句主语的一部分或者跟它相关。

In sentences with a subject-predicate phrase as the predicate, the structure is "subject of the sentence＋predicate of the sentence (subject＋predicate)", and the subject in the subject-predicate phrase is usually part of the subject of the sentence or related to it.

例如 Example

（1）今天天气不错。

（2）他身体怎么样？

（3）你肚子饿不饿？（电影原句）

综合练习 Comprehensive Exercises

一、选择恰当的词语填空并朗读 Choose the Proper Words to Fill in the Blanks and Read the Sentences Aloud

之后　意外　伸　安全　控制

❶ 他________手去拿那本书。

❷ 天黑了，路上注意________。

❸ 听说他住院了，我们都觉得很________。

❹ 这种事不是我能________的。

❺ 去中国________我的汉语越来越好了。

二、听后重复句子 Repeat after Listening

三、判断对错 Ture or False

❶ 周小狄考试得了六十分。　（　　）

❷ 周爸爸被送到医院了。　（　　）

❸ 周爸爸还活着。　（　　）

❹ 是袁老师送周小狄回的家。　（　　）

四、连词成句 Rearrange the Words or Phrases to Make Sentences

❶ 这　一个　其实　意外　只是 →

② 自己的　人　控制　可以　心情 →
③ 服务员　之后　十点　上班　开始 →
④ 安全带　系　请　好 →

五、看图造句 Make Sentences According to the Pictures

搬

醒

______________　　　______________

六、回答问题 Answer the Questions

① 周爸爸出了什么意外？
② 七仔对周爸爸做了什么？结果怎么样？

七、角色配音 Role Play

两人一组，分别扮演周小狄和袁老师。

八、中文脱口秀 Chinese Talk Show（2.5分钟）

生活中我们应该怎样注意安全？

提示：水、电、天然气、饮食、出行、钱财等。

文化知识 Cultural Knowledge

反串表演

Cross-dressing Performance

《长江七号》中的周小狄、蛋挞头、美娇、暴龙都是反串表演。反串本是中国国粹京剧的一种演出方式，指演员不出演平时固定的角色类型，而出演其他角色类型，如生角扮丑角、丑角扮净角等（京剧里的人物分为生、旦、净、末、丑五种）。现今影视界的反串是指男扮女或女扮男的表演，即扮演与自己性别不一致的角色。较为经典的反串角色有叶童在电视剧《新白娘子传奇》中饰演的许仙、林青霞在电影《笑傲江湖》中饰演的东方不败等。

In *CJ7*, Zhou Xiaodi, "Egg Tart", Mei Jiao and "Tyrannosaurus" are all cross-dressing performances. This is a kind of performance in Peking Opera, the quintessence of Chinese culture. It means that actors do not play the usual fixed role types, but play other roles, such as "Sheng" play "Chou", or "Chou" plays "Jing". The characters in Peking Opera are divided into Sheng, Dan, Jing, Mo and Chou. Cross-dressing in today's film and television industry refers to acting as a man or a woman disguised as a man, playing a role that is not consistent with one's gender. Some of the classic cross-characters are Xu Xian played by Ye Tong in the TV series *The New Legend of White Snake*, and Dongfang Bubai played by Lin Qingxia in the movie *The Swordsman*.

第二十二课　重生 Back to Life

（电影片段 73：56—80：32）

生词 Words/Phrases

1. 听话	tīng huà	adj.	be tractable，be obedient
2. 社会	shèhuì	n.	society
3. 声音	shēngyīn	n.	sound，voice

语法点 Grammar Notes

1 连动句（连谓句）

连动句是由两个动词短语共同充当谓语的句子，也可以由连动短语直接构成句子。连动句的动词在意义上有目的、方式、因果等关系，顺序不能互换，中间也没有语音停顿。

In some Chinese sentences，two verb phrases can form together as predicates of a sentence，or a sentence which is called continuous predicate sentence. The function of the verbs in these sentences usually are to express purpose，method，and causality，etc. The order of the verbs in the continuous predicate sentence cannot be interchanged，and there is no sound pause between them.

例如 Example

（1）我**去教室学习**。

（2）他**用铅笔写字**。

（3）奶奶**生病住院**了。

（4）为什么不**换衣服睡觉**？（电影原句）

2 双重否定句

双重否定句中使用两个否定副词来表示肯定的意义，如“不要不”“不能不”“不会不”“不得不”“没有……不”等。双重否定句有加强或弱化语气的作用。

Double negative adverbs, such as “不要不” “不能不” “不会不” “不得不” “没有……不”, can be used in a sentence which is called the double negative sentence, to express affirmative meaning. The function of the double negative sentences is to strengthen or weaken the tone.

例如 Example

(1) 你是我的朋友，我**不会不**帮你。

(2) 你**不能不**吃蔬菜。

(3) 已经很晚了，我**不得不**回家了。

(4) 她又聪明又漂亮，**没有**人**不**喜欢她。

(5) 爸爸，你**不要不**管我。(电影原句)

综合练习 Comprehensive Exercises

一、选择恰当的词语填空并朗读 Choose the Proper Words to Fill in the Blanks and Read the Sentences Aloud

社会　声音　听话

1. 这个孩子太不________了。
2. ________上好人比坏人多。
3. 你听，这是妈妈的________吗？

二、听后重复句子 Repeat after Listening

三、判断对错 Ture or False

❶ 周小狄睡醒后看见了爸爸。 （　）

❷ 周小狄不想爸爸管自己。 （　）

❸ 七仔还和以前一样。 （　）

❹ 周爸爸觉得七仔可能没电了。 （　）

四、连词成句 Rearrange the Words or Phrases to Make Sentences

❶ 面包　姐姐　商店　去　买→

❷ 不　他　不会　知道　这件事→

❸ 听话的　一个　弟弟　是　孩子→

❹ 大　声音　电视的　太　了→

五、看图造句 Make Sentence According to the Picture

听话

____

六、回答问题 Answer the Questions

❶ 七仔怎么了？为什么？

❷ 周爸爸对七仔做了什么？结果怎么样？

七、角色配音 Role Play

两人一组，分别扮演周爸爸和周小狄。

八、中文脱口秀 Chinese Talk Show（2.5分钟）

周小狄在七仔变成玩偶之后做了什么？

文化知识 Cultural Knowledge

“仔”字的含义
The Meaning of the Word“仔”

“仔”有“青年”的意思，在广东、广西方言中可以用来称呼小孩、青年人、小动物等，比如小男孩可以叫“细路仔”，自己的孩子可以叫“仔仔”（一般用于男孩），年轻男孩可以叫“靓仔”，男性后辈可以叫“后生仔”；“仔”也可以称呼具有某种特征或从事某种职业的年轻男性，比如“肥仔”“打工仔”等。另外，“崽”字也可以用于小孩、幼小的动物，但有时有贬义。

Character“仔（zǎi）”has the meaning of “young，immature”，in dialect of Guangdong and Guangxi，it can be used to address children，teenagers，animals，etc. For example，boys can be called“细路仔（xìlùzǎi）”. Their own children can be called“仔仔（zǎizǎi）”for boys. Young boys can be called“靓仔（liàngzǎi）”. Male successors can be called“后生仔（hòushēngzǎi）”. “仔”can also be used to refer to young men with certain characteristics or occupations，such as“肥仔（féizǎi）”（fat boy）and“打工仔（dǎgōngzǎi）”（laborer/employee）. In addition，the word“崽（zǎi）”can also be used for children，young animals，but sometimes has a derogatory meaning.

第二十三课　七仔回来了 CJ7 Came Back

（电影片段 80：33—84：13）

生词 Words/Phrases

1. 学期	xuéqī	n.	term，semester
2. 特地	tèdì	adv.	specially，for a particular purpose
3. 旅行	lǚxíng	v.	to travel，to tour
4. 开心	kāixīn	adj.	happy，glad
5. 却	què	adv.	but，yet
6. 例外	lìwài	n.	exception
7. 神奇	shénqí	adj.	magical，miraculous
8. 躺	tǎng	v.	to lie (on one's back)
9. 后来	hòulái	n.	later，afterwards
10. 明白	míngbai	v. /adj.	to know；clear
11. 解释	jiěshì	v.	to explain
12. 英俊	yīngjùn	adj.	handsome
13. 好笑	hǎoxiào	adj.	funny，laughable
14. 容易	róngyì	adj.	easy
15. 放弃	fàngqì	v.	to give up
16. 清楚	qīngchu	adj.	clear，distinct
17. 自从	zìcóng	prep.	ever since
18. 闭	bì	v.	to close，to shut
19. 数	shǔ	v.	to count
20. 睁	zhēng	v.	to open one's eyes
21. 诚意	chéngyì	n.	sincerity，bonafide

语法点 Grammar Notes

1 副词“再”

副词“再”可以放在动词前边，表示还没发生的重复动作或情况，也可用来表示某个动作将要在某种情况下出现。

The adverb “再” can be put before a verb to indicate the recurrence of an action or a situation has not happened yet, it can also indicate that an action will happen under a certain circumstance.

例如 Example

（1）你吃得很少，**再**吃一点儿。

（2）面包不多了，**再**买一点儿吧。

（3）我吃完饭**再**去上课。

（4）暴龙同学不**再**打架了。（电影原句）

2 动词“上”

动词“上”可以用在动词后做趋向补语，引申表示动作行为达到了目的；或者做可能补语，表示动作行为能否达到目的。

The verb “上” is used after another verb as a complement of direction, indicating the purpose of an action or a behavior has been achieved, or as a complement of possibility, showing whether or not the purpose of an action or a behavior can be achieved.

例如 Example

（1）哥哥考**上**了大学。

（2）今天吃不**上**她做的菜了。

（3）因为他喜欢**上**了一个人。（电影原句）

3 副词“却”

副词“却”用于主语后、动词或形容词前，表示转折，语气比较轻。

The adverb “却” is used after the subject and before the verb or adjective to indicate a transition in meaning in a softer tone.

例如 Example

（1）我们是同学，**却**没说过话。

（2）她不吃羊肉饺子，但**却**吃涮羊肉。

（3）爷爷九十多岁了，**却**很健康。

（4）但美娇**却**喜欢我。（电影原句）

4 疑问代词“多”

疑问代词“多”可用在形容词前，一般对程度进行提问，或用在否定性陈述句中。

The interrogative pronoun “多” is used before an adjective, asking about the degree of something. “多” also can be used in negative declarative sentences.

例如 Example

（1）你**多**大了？

（2）哥哥**多**高？

（3）我就告诉老师，看你们能好**多**久。（电影原句）

综合练习 Comprehensive Exercises

一、选择恰当的词语填空并朗读 Choose the Proper Words to Fill in the Blanks and Read the Sentences Aloud

例外　却　后来　躺　特地

❶ 这是我________为你买的巧克力。

❷ 弟弟想出去玩，妈妈________不让。

❸ 所有学生都要按时完成作业，谁也不能________。

❹ 她在床上________了一天。

❺ 刚开始我觉得有点儿热，________就不热了。

英俊　放弃　容易　数　自从

❻ 他长得非常________。

❼ 这个问题很________回答。

❽ 只要还有希望，我就不会________。

❾ ________认识她，哥哥就每天给她打电话。

❿ 请________一下一共有多少人。

二、听后重复句子 Repeat after Listening

三、判断对错 Ture or False

❶ 暴龙同学还经常打架。 (　　)

❷ 小芬很喜欢蛋挞头。 (　　)

❸ 袁老师没觉得周爸爸很英俊。 (　　)

❹ 飞碟上有很多不同颜色的七仔。 (　　)

四、连词成句 Rearrange the Words or Phrases to Make Sentences

❶ 吗　再说　你　能　一遍 →

❷ 他　篮球　上了　喜欢　打 →

❸ 床　长　张　那　多 →

❹ 没　明白　我　这道题　听 →

五、看图造句 Make Sentences According to the Pictures

解释

____

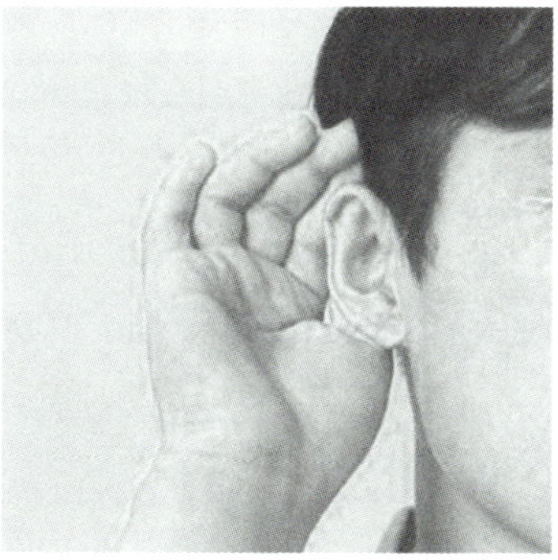

清楚

____

六、回答问题 Answer the Questions

❶ 你觉得周小狄这个人怎么样？

❷ 你觉得周爸爸这个人怎么样？

❸ 你觉得袁老师这个人怎么样？

七、角色配音 Role Play

三人一组，分别扮演周小狄、周爸爸和袁老师。

八、中文脱口秀 Chinese Talk Show（2.5分钟）

你对这部电影有什么看法？

文化知识 Cultural Knowledge

中国的科幻电影

Chinese science fiction movies

中国第一部科幻电影可能是拍摄于20世纪60年代的《小太阳》，八九十年代又有《珊瑚岛上的死光》《霹雳贝贝》《错位》《大气层消失》等经典科幻电影。2019年，根据刘慈欣同名小说改编的“硬科幻”电影《流浪地球》上映，其中国内地票房超46亿元，并获得中国电影金鸡奖。《流浪地球》被誉为中国科幻电影的里程碑。

China's first science fiction film was probably *Little Sun*, which was made in the 1960s. In the 1980s and 1990s, there were classic sci-fi films such as *Death-Pay on Coral Island*, *Thunderbolt Baby*, *Dislocated* and *The Atmosphere Layer Vanishes*. In 2019, a hard science fiction film *The Wandering Earth*, which based on Liu Cixin's novel of the same name, made more than 4.6 billion Yuan. It has won the Golden Rooster Awards. *The Wandering Earth* has been hailed as a milestone in Chinese science fiction films.

附录 1　听力文本 Listening Materials

第一课

1. 今天怎么这么热？
2. 他走过来了。
3. 我刚才去商店了。
4. 谁汉语说得好？
5. 你的妈妈是做什么工作的？
6. 请把桌子擦干净。
7. 等你有时间的时候就告诉我。

第二课

1. 弟弟的志愿是当电影明星。
2. 我的手机被谁拿走了？
3. 只要努力学习，就能学好汉语。
4. 就算天气冷，他也要出去跑步。
5. 虽然他很穷，但是他有骨气。
6. 我觉得哪里都不舒服。
7. 学生要尊敬老师。

第三课

1. 天气越来越热了。
2. 她越来越喜欢打乒乓球。
3. 我想找时间去看看他。
4. 昨天我们听了听音乐。
5. 你这么早就起床吗？

6. 弟弟在睡觉。
7. 世界上有几千种语言。

第四课

1. 他被老师罚站了。
2. 对不起，我不是故意的。
3. 这双鞋是破的，请换一双。
4. 苹果是我买的。
5. 哥哥很喜欢上体育课。
6. 所有菜都很好吃。
7. 我想永远陪着你。

第五课

1. 天气太热了，我想歇一会儿。
2. 姐姐吃不了这么多水果。
3. 买苹果不如买西瓜。
4. 先洗澡，再睡觉。
5. 我听得见他的话。
6. 这两本书有很大分别。
7. 我朋友的学习能力很强。

第六课

1. 明天是阴天还是晴天？
2. 房间里有几十把椅子。
3. 你很喜欢打篮球，是不是？
4. 虽然汉字有点儿难，但是很有意思。
5. 他跑完步就去洗澡了。
6. 今年终于下雪了。
7. 先向前走，再往右转。

第七课

1. 请你等我一下。

2. 他长得高高的。
3. 你吃过什么中国菜？
4. 最近我走路去上班。
5. 当时我正在洗衣服。
6. 他好像后天过生日。
7. 这个相机有很多功能。

第八课

1. 爸爸晚上十一点还在工作。
2. 我觉得这个宾馆还不错。
3. 运动对身体好。
4. 这个手机贵不贵？
5. 今天我刚好有时间。
6. 教育孩子不能单靠老师。
7. 她经常和女儿沟通。

第九课

1. 请把笔拿过去。
2. 我把钱花完了。
3. 西瓜比苹果贵一些。
4. 老师穿着白色的衣服。
5. 他每天晚上加班。
6. 不许乱扔垃圾。
7. 你一定认识她。

第十课

1. 她找到妈妈了。
2. 我没听懂老师的话。
3. 他的房间好大。
4. 那本书我看了两遍。
5. 这个话题很有意思。
6. 我不信他是大学生。

7. 别把衣服挂起来。

第十一课

1. 如果你喜欢，我就给你买。
2. 这是他的第四本汉语书。
3. 我喝过三次绿茶。
4. 明天有考试，我要复习复习。
5. 哥哥今天没戴眼镜。
6. 上个星期他的手受伤了。
7. 这次我的考试成绩不错。

第十二课

1. 她的丈夫就要回来了。
2. 老师叫我努力学习。
3. 他果然会做中国菜。
4. 我踢足球没有天分。
5. 这几天我的睡眠不充足。
6. 你需要开车吗？
7. 这件事她做得很合情理。

第十三课

1. 今天不是下雨吗？怎么没下？
2. 别玩手机了，对眼睛不好。
3. 时间怎么过得这么快？
4. 他经常和别人开玩笑。
5. 弟弟在认真地写作业。
6. 我能试一试这双鞋吗？
7. 这是我最后的机会。

第十四课

1. 我的小猫呢？
2. 他是和我一起旅游的同学。

3. 原来你们是夫妻。
4. 别眨眼，认真看。
5. 这瓶水的盖子不见了。
6. 给你一千块钱够不够？
7. 我不知道是什么缘故。

第十五课

1. 你什么时候去呀？
2. 哥哥长得真高哇。
3. 你要小心哪！
4. 那个书包不是我的。
5. 请把椅子拉出来。
6. 他跑了，快去追！
7. 这个苹果可以直接吃，不用洗。

第十六课

1. 你中过彩票吗？
2. 他到底几点能来？
3. 坐飞机要八个小时呢。
4. 这些书全是我的。
5. 她是一个聪明的孩子。
6. 别伤心了，我们会帮你。
7. 前年这家饭店着火了。

第十七课

1. 姐姐喝的明明是茶，不是咖啡。
2. 早睡才能早起。
3. 这个女孩儿很了不起。
4. 考试的时候不要作弊。
5. 事情不是这样，你不要胡说。
6. 我很长时间没用墨水了。
7. 我的电脑和他的一样。

第十八课

1. 你几点回来都行，反正我在家。
2. 天气冷就多穿衣服。
3. 他是个很老实的人，不会做那种事。
4. 昨天的考试结果怎么样？
5. 她自己给自己过生日。
6. 开出租车非常辛苦。
7. 今天的事情让他觉得很烦。

第十九课

1. 你这样做，她会不高兴的。
2. 大家还有什么问题吗？
3. 妹妹出生那天正好下雪。
4. 今天王先生忘了买早饭。
5. 请把你们的功课交给我。
6. 他又和同学闹别扭了。
7. 你介意我坐在这里吗？

第二十课

1. 要是明天天气不好我就不去了。
2. 已经九点了，赶快起床吧。
3. 他是我的大学同学，也是我的同乡。
4. 这个东西我要当面送给李小姐。
5. 这是你的生日礼物，请收下。
6. 过年的时候很多人会发红包。
7. 这几天她很不走运。

第二十一课

1. 今天 1 月 17 号，星期日。
2. 你过来。
3. 西瓜很便宜。

4. 奶奶身体不太好。
5. 他考试没及格。
6. 你睡醒了吗?
7. 别把头伸出去。

第二十二课

1. 他开门出去了。
2. 人不能不喝水。
3. 你应该听妈妈的话。
4. 现在社会上工作机会很多。
5. 妹妹的声音很好听。

第二十三课

1. 现在还早，我再睡一会儿。
2. 妹妹穿上了绿色的衣服。
3. 我不认识他，他却认识我。
4. 你来中国多久了?
5. 下个学期我会去旅行。
6. 今天她有点儿不开心。
7. 现在闭上眼，一分钟以后再睁开。

附录 2　词汇总表 Vocabulary

词性 Parts of Speech	英文简称 Abbreviations	词性 Parts of Speech	英文简称 Abbreviations
名词	n.	介词	prep.
动词	v.	连词	conj.
形容词	adj.	助词	part.
副词	adv.	叹词	int.
代词	pron.	拟声词	onom.
数词	num.	前缀	pref.
量词	m.	后缀	suf.

词语 Words/Phrases	拼音 Pinyin	词性 Parts of Speech	词义 Meanings	课号 Lesson
			A	
啊	a	part.	used at the end of a sentence to indicate confirmation or defense	1
矮	ǎi	adj.	short	3
安全	ānquán	adj.	safe，secure	21
			B	
把	bǎ	prep. /m.	function words；used for things with a handle	1
被	bèi	prep.	used to indicate the passive voice	2
不过	búguò	conj.	but，yet	4
不如	bùrú	v.	to be not as good as，to be inferior to	5
殡葬	bìnzàng	n.	funeral	5
爆	bào	v.	to explode，to burst	6
补	bǔ	v.	to repair，to patch	6
不然	bùrán	conj.	or else，otherwise	6

续表 1

词语 Words/Phrases	拼音 Pinyin	词性 Parts of Speech	词义 Meanings	课号 Lesson
报道	bàodào	v. /n.	to report; report	7
比较	bǐjiào	adv.	fairly, rather	8
遍	biàn	m.	(denoting an action from beginning to end) time	10
逼	bī	v.	to force, to compel	10
巴掌	bāzhang	n.	palm	10
变魔术	biàn móshù	phr.	to perform magic tricks, to conjure	10
帮忙	bāng máng	v.	to help	11
包	bāo	n.	bag, sack	15
本事	běnshi	n.	ability, capability	18
报答	bàodá	v.	to pay back	19
搬	bān	v.	to carry, to move	21
闭	bì	v.	to close, to shut	23
			C	
擦	cā	v.	to wipe	1
吹牛	chuī niú	v.	to boast, to brag	2
超级	chāojí	adj.	super	3
长江	Cháng Jiāng	n.	Yangtze River	3
成	chéng	v.	used before a complement of result; to become	3
才	cái	adv.	just	3
吵	chǎo	v. /adj.	to make a noise; noisy	10
苍蝇	cāngying	n.	fly	11
成绩	chéngjì	n.	grade, achievement	11
充足	chōngzú	adj.	ample, sufficient	12
创	chuàng	v.	to create, to produce	12
差劲	chàjìn	adj.	disappointing, bad	13
充	chōng	v.	to fill	14
聪明	cōngmíng	adj.	clever, smart	16
彩票	cǎipiào	n.	lottery ticket	16
臭	chòu	adj.	smelly, stinking	20

续表 2

词语 Words/Phrases	拼音 Pinyin	词性 Parts of Speech	词义 Meanings	课号 Lesson
诚意	chéngyì	n.	sincerity, bonafide	23
		D		
当	dāng	v. /prep.	to become; when	2
打架	dǎ jià	v.	to fight, come to blows	2
低	dī	adj.	low	3
带	dài	v.	to take along, to bring	4
德行	déxing	n.	appearance	5
顶	dǐng	v. /n.	to be qualified; to go against; top	5
地	dì	n.	ground	5
肚子	dùzi	n.	belly, stomach	6
动画片	dònghuàpiàn	n.	animated cartoon	7
当时	dāngshí	n.	then, at that time	7
单	dān	adv.	only, solely	8
掉	diào	v.	used after certain verbs, indicating the result of an action	9
灯	dēng	n.	light, lamp	10
丢	diū	v.	to throw, to cast; to lose	10
地球	dìqiú	n.	earth, globe	10
打败	dǎbài	v.	to defeat	11
戴	dài	v.	to wear (accessories)	11
到底	dàodǐ	adv.	(used in question for emphasis) on earth	16
当然	dāngrán	adv.	of course	16
队	duì	n.	team	16
当面	dāng miàn	adv.	to one's face, in one's presence	20
带	dài	n.	belt	21
		E		
而已	éryǐ	part.	nothing more, only	4
饿	è	adj.	hungry	6
而	ér	conj.	and; furthermore; while	13
		F		
方面	fāngmiàn	n.	aspect	2

续表3

词语 Words/Phrases	拼音 Pinyin	词性 Parts of Speech	词义 Meanings	课号 Lesson
放	fàng	v.	to put, to place; to release	2
罚站	fázhàn	v.	to stand for a punishment	4
风扇	fēngshàn	n.	electric fan	5
费	fèi	n.	cost	5
副	fù	m.	pair; set	5
分别	fēnbié	n. /adv.	difference; respectively	5
飞行	fēixíng	v.	to fly	7
飞碟	fēidié	n.	flying saucer (UFO)	7
方便	fāngbiàn	adj.	convenient	7
发	fā	v.	to send out, to launch	7
发财	fā cái	v.	to be rich	10
复习	fùxí	v.	to review	11
疯	fēng	adj.	crazy, mad	12
法宝	fǎbǎo	n.	magic weapon	13
风	fēng	n.	wind	13
烦	fán	adj.	vexed, annoyed	18
反正	fǎnzhèng	adv.	anyway, no matter what	18
放心	fàng xīn	v.	to ease one's mind, to rest assured	19
放弃	fàngqì	v.	to give up	23
G				
刚才	gāngcái	n.	just now	1
干净	gānjìng	adj.	clean	1
跟	gēn	prep. /v. /conj.	with; to follow; and	1
骨气	gǔqì	n.	moral integrity, strength of character	2
共同	gòngtóng	adv. /adj.	together; common	3
干吗	gànmá	pron.	what to do; why	3
怪物	guàiwu	n.	monster, freak	3
故意	gùyì	adv.	intentionally, on purpose	4
盖	gài	v.	to build; to cover	5

续表 4

词语 Words/Phrases	拼音 Pinyin	词性 Parts of Speech	词义 Meanings	课号 Lesson
供	gòng	v.	to supply	5
贵族	guìzú	n.	noble	5
关于	guānyú	prep.	about, regarding	7
工资	gōngzī	n.	pay, salary	7
功能	gōngnéng	n.	function	7
乖	guāi	adj.	obedient, well-behaved	8
刚好	gānghǎo	adv.	by coincidence	8
沟通	gōutōng	v.	to communicate	8
挂	guà	v.	to hang, to put up	10
关	guān	v.	to lock, to close, to turn off	10
敢	gǎn	v.	to dare	10
果然	guǒrán	adv.	as expected, really	12
过分	guòfèn	adj.	excessive	12
过头	guòtóu	adj.	excessive, undue	12
盖子	gàizi	n.	lid, cover	14
够	gòu	v.	to be enough	14
工具	gōngjù	n.	tool, instrument	15
干	gàn	v.	to do, to act	16
光	guāng	adj. /n.	nothing left, all gone; light	16
滚	gǔn	v.	to get out; to roll	17
骨头	gǔtou	n.	bone	17
改	gǎi	v.	to change, to modify	17
搞	gǎo	v.	(followed by a complement) to produce a certain effect or result	18
管	guǎn	v.	to manage, to administer	18
功课	gōngkè	n.	schoolwork, homework, lesson	19
感谢	gǎnxiè	v.	to thank	19
赶快	gǎnkuài	adv.	hurriedly	20
H				
换	huàn	v.	to change, to substitute	4

续表5

词语 Words/Phrases	拼音 Pinyin	词性 Parts of Speech	词义 Meanings	课号 Lesson
还	huán	v.	to return	5
还是	háishi	conj.	or	6
好端端	hǎoduānduān	adj.	in good condition, when everything is all right	6
怀疑	huáiyí	v.	to suspect, to doubt	7
好像	hǎoxiàng	adv.	as if	7
坏	huài	adj.	bad, broken	7
话题	huàtí	n.	topic	10
合	hé	v.	to unite, to combine	12
合情理	hé qínglǐ	phr.	within reason	12
活该	huógāi	adj.	deserving	13
还原	huán yuán	v.	to restore to the original state or shape	14
盒	hé	n.	box, case	14
胡说	húshuō	v.	to talk nonsense	17
红包	hóngbāo	n.	red envelop, lucky money	20
后来	hòulái	n.	later, afterwards	23
好笑	hǎoxiào	adj.	funny, laughable	23
			J	
借口	jièkǒu	n.	excuse	1
见面	jiàn miàn	v.	to meet	1
就算	jiùsuàn	conj.	even if	2
警察	jǐngchá	n.	police	3
捡	jiǎn	v.	to pick up, to collect	4
劲(儿)	jìn(r)	n.	strength	5
将来	jiānglái	n.	future	5
假	jiǎ	adj.	false, fake	6
旧	jiù	adj.	old, used, worn	6
机灵	jīling	adj.	smart	6
尽力	jìn lì	v.	to try one's best	6
进步	jìnbù	n./v.	progress; to make a progress	6
简称	jiǎnchēng	v./n.	for short; abbreviation	7

续表 6

词语 Words/Phrases	拼音 Pinyin	词性 Parts of Speech	词义 Meanings	课号 Lesson
家访	jiāfǎng	v.	to visit the parents of school-children	8
教育	jiàoyù	v. /n.	to educate; education	8
加班	jiā bān	v.	to work overtime	9
救	jiù	v.	to save, to rescue	10
检查	jiǎnchá	v.	to check, to examine	11
纪录	jìlù	n. /v.	record, note; to record, to note down	12
叫	jiào	v.	to let	12
机会	jīhuì	n.	opportunity	13
境界	jìngjiè	n.	extent, degree	13
借	jiè	v.	to borrow, to lend	14
锯	jù	v. /n.	to saw; saw	15
加入	jiārù	v.	to join, to accede	16
贱	jiàn	adj.	cheap, lowly	17
久	jiǔ	adj.	for a long time, long	17
结果	jiéguǒ	n.	result	18
交	jiāo	v.	to give, to hand in/over	19
介意	jiè yì	v.	to mind	19
缴	jiǎo	v.	to pay	20
及格	jí gé	v.	to pass a exam	21
解释	jiěshì	v.	to explain	23
		K		
科学家	kēxuéjiā	n.	scientist	3
哭	kū	v.	to cry	8
靠	kào	v.	to rely on, to depend on; to lean against	8
恐怖	kǒngbù	adj.	terrible, horrible	10
肯定	kěndìng	adv.	surely, certainly	10
科技	kējì	n.	science and technology	13
肯	kěn	v.	be willing to	19
口	kǒu	n. /m.	mouth; used for members of families	20

续表7

词语 Words/Phrases	拼音 Pinyin	词性 Parts of Speech	词义 Meanings	课号 Lesson
开工	kāi gōng	v.	to start working	20
控制	kòngzhì	v.	to control，to take command of	21
开心	kāixīn	adj.	happy，glad	23
		L		
老	lǎo	adv. /adj.	always；old	1
另外	lìngwài	pron. /conj.	other；besides，in addition	3
啦	la	part.	combination of the sound of 了 and 啊，expressing exclamation，interrogation，etc.	3
理	lǐ	v.	to respond	3
老板	lǎobǎn	n.	boss，employer	5
老婆	lǎopo	n.	wife	5
乱	luàn	adv. /adj.	random；disordered；confused	6
厉害	lìhai	adj.	awesome，serious	9
垃圾	lājī	n.	rubbish，garbage	9
烂	làn	adj.	rotten，putrid	10
冷静	lěngjìng	adj.	calm，composed	12
拉	lā	v.	to pull，to drag	15
了不起	liǎobuqǐ	adj.	great，amazing	17
老实	lǎoshi	adj.	honest，frank	18
赖皮	làipí	v.	to renegue	18
旅行	lǚxíng	v.	to travel，to tour	23
例外	lìwài	n.	exception	23
		M		
民工	míngōng	n.	farmer-laborer	1
明星	míngxīng	n.	star，celebrity	2
嘛	ma	part.	to indicata that the reason is obvious	5
马上	mǎshàng	adv.	immediately，at once	7
命	mìng	n.	life	10
梦	mèng	n.	dream	12
秘密	mìmì	n. /adj.	secret	16

续表 8

词语 Words/Phrases	拼音 Pinyin	词性 Parts of Speech	词义 Meanings	课号 Lesson
蛮	mán	adv.	very, quite	16
墨水	mòshuǐ	n.	ink	17
明明	míngmíng	adv.	obviously, undoubtedly	17
明白	míngbai	v. /adj.	to know; clear	23
		N		
弄	nòng	v.	to make, to do	1
拿	ná	v.	to take, to fetch	1
努力	nǔlì	adj.	hard-working	2
能力	nénglì	n.	ability, competence	5
念	niàn	v.	to read	6
难度	nándù	n.	difficulty	12
难道	nándào	adv.	used in a rhetorical question for emphasis	13
能耐	néngnai	n.	ability, capability	18
闹别扭	nào bièniu	phr.	be at odds with, be difficult with	19
内疚	nèijiù	adj.	compunctious, guilty	19
		P		
片酬	piānchóu	n.	remuneration for a movie actor/actress	2
碰	pèng	v.	to touch; to meet	2
陪	péi	v.	to accompany	4
破	pò	adj.	broken, torn	4
普通	pǔtōng	adj.	common	5
凭	píng	v. /prep.	to rely on; on the basis of	5
拍	pāi	v.	to take (a photo), to shoot (a video)	7
牌子	páizi	n.	brand	7
脾气	píqi	n.	temper, disposition	8
骗	piàn	v.	to cheat, to deceive	10
怕	pà	v.	to be afraid, to be scared	10
拼	pīn	v.	to put up a desperate fight	13
品味	pǐnwèi	n. /v.	taste; to taste	13

续表9

词语 Words/Phrases	拼音 Pinyin	词性 Parts of Speech	词义 Meanings	课号 Lesson
			Q	
去世	qùshì	v.	pass away	1
企业家	qǐyèjiā	n.	enterpriser, entrepreneur	2
穷	qióng	adj.	poor, impoverished	2
枪毙	qiāngbì	v.	to execute by shooting	3
欺负	qīfu	v.	to bully	3
穷鬼	qióngguǐ	n.	pauper, the poor	3
其实	qíshí	adv.	actually	4
强	qiáng	adj.	strong	5
抢	qiǎng	v.	to rob	6
情况	qíngkuàng	n.	situation, circumstance	7
求	qiú	v.	to beg	7
侵略	qīnlüè	v.	to invade, to aggress	10
趣味	qùwèi	n.	interest, delight	13
全	quán	adj.	all, whole	16
却	què	adv.	but, yet	23
清楚	qīngchu	adj.	clear, distinct	23
			R	
扔	rēng	v.	to throw away	9
如果	rúguǒ	conj.	if, in case	11
认真	rènzhēn	adj.	serious, earnest	13
人才	réncái	n.	talented person, person with ability	14
柔道	róudào	n.	judo, jiujitsu	16
容易	róngyì	adj.	easy	23
			S	
摔跤	shuāi jiāo	v.	fall down	1
受到	shòudào	v.	to receive	2
世界	shìjiè	n.	world	3
素质	sùzhì	n.	quality	3
死	sǐ	v. /adj.	to die; dead	3

续表 10

词语 Words/Phrases	拼音 Pinyin	词性 Parts of Speech	词义 Meanings	课号 Lesson
所有	suǒyǒu	adj.	all	4
双	shuāng	m.	pair	4
散工	sǎngōng	n.	casual laborer	5
水泥	shuǐní	n.	cement	5
扇	shàn	n.	fan	6
耍	shuǎ	v.	to cheat, to play, to behave (in an unsavory manner)	6
属于	shǔyú	v.	to belong to	6
时代	shídài	n.	era, age, epoch	6
嗖	sōu	onom.	whoosh	7
声响	shēngxiǎng	n.	sound, voice	7
算了	suànle	part.	forget it, never mind, let it be	9
受伤	shòu shāng	v.	to be hurt, to be injured	11
睡眠	shuìmián	n.	sleep	12
傻	shǎ	adj.	stupid, foolish	13
试	shì	v.	to try	13
生气	shēng qì	v.	to get angry	13
随	suí	v.	to follow, along with	13
说谎	shuō huǎng	v.	to lie	14
伤心	shāng xīn	adj.	sad, sorrowful	16
收	shōu	v.	to take, to receive	20
伸	shēn	v.	to stretch, to extend	21
社会	shèhuì	n.	society	22
声音	shēngyīn	n.	sound, voice	22
神奇	shénqí	adj.	magical, miraculous	23
数	shǔ	v.	to count	23
T				
体育	tǐyù	n.	P. E. , sports	4
退	tuì	v.	to go back	6
偷	tōu	v.	to steal	6

续表11

词语 Words/Phrases	拼音 Pinyin	词性 Parts of Speech	词义 Meanings	课号 Lesson
挺	tǐng	adv.	quite, rather	8
头	tóu	n.	head	9
桶	tǒng	n.	barrel, bucket	9
调皮	tiáopí	adj.	naughty, mischievous	10
甜	tián	adj.	sweet	10
太空	tàikōng	n.	outer space	11
天分	tiānfèn	n.	talent, genius	12
坨	tuó	m.	lump	13
疼	téng	v. /adj.	to love dearly; hurt, painful	13
捅	tǒng	v.	to stab	13
坦白	tǎnbái	v.	to confess	13
弹力	tánlì	n.	elasticity	14
谈	tán	v.	to talk, to discuss	19
同乡	tóngxiāng	n.	a person from the same hometown or province	20
听话	tīng huà	adj.	be tractable, be obedient	22
特地	tèdì	adv.	specially, for a particular purpose	23
躺	tǎng	v.	to lie (on one's back)	23
		W		
玩具	wánjù	n.	toy	3
物体	wùtǐ	n.	object	7
玩意儿	wányìr	n.	thing, stuff	7
丸	wán	n.	bolus	10
尾巴	wěiba	n.	tail	10
玩笑	wánxiào	n.	joke	13
误会	wùhuì	v. /n.	to misunderstand; misunderstanding	13
忘	wàng	v.	to forget	19
温习	wēnxí	v.	to review	19
		X		
小心	xiǎoxīn	adj.	careful	1
吓	xià	v.	to frighten, to scare	3

续表 12

词语 Words/Phrases	拼音 Pinyin	词性 Parts of Speech	词义 Meanings	课号 Lesson
鞋	xié	n.	shoe	4
歇	xiē	v.	to rest，to take a rest	5
先	xiān	adv.	first，in advance	5
详细	xiángxì	adj.	detailed	7
相机	xiàngjī	n.	camera	7
（相）信	（xiāng）xìn	v.	to believe	10
像	xiàng	v.	to be like	10
星	xīng	n.	star，planet	10
新鲜	xīnxiān	adj.	fresh	10
凶恶	xiōng'è	adj.	atrocious，ferocious	11
需要	xūyào	v.	to need	12
幸运	xìngyùn	adj.	lucky，fortunate	14
箱	xiāng	n.	box，bin	15
辛苦	xīnkǔ	adj.	hard，toilsome	18
嚣张	xiāozhāng	adj.	arrogant，rampant	18
醒	xǐng	v.	to wake up，to be awake	21
学期	xuéqī	n.	term，semester	23
			Y	
研究	yánjiū	v.	to research，to study	3
样子	yàngzi	n.	look，appearance	3
有用	yǒuyòng	adj.	useful，helpful	3
英雄	yīngxióng	n.	hero	3
呀	ya	part.	a variant of the interjection 啊	4
永远	yǒngyuǎn	adv.	forever	4
一辈子	yībèizi	n.	all one's life	5
摇晃	yáohuàng	v. /adj.	to shake；shaky	7
一直	yīzhí	adv.	all the time	8
一定	yīdìng	adv.	definitely，certainly	9
（允）许	（yǔn）xǔ	v.	to allow，to permit	9

续表13

词语 Words/Phrases	拼音 Pinyin	词性 Parts of Speech	词义 Meanings	课号 Lesson
(要)不然	(yào)bùrán	conj.	otherwise, or else	9
眼镜	yǎnjìng	n.	glasses, spectacles	11
腰	yāo	n.	waist	12
冤枉	yuānwang	v.	to treat unjustly	13
应该	yīnggāi	v.	should	13
以为	yǐwéi	v.	to think, to believe	13
以后	yǐhòu	n.	after, hereafter	14
原来	yuánlái	adv. /adj.	so that is how it is; original	14
缘故	yuángù	n.	cause, reason	14
烟花	yānhuā	n.	firework	16
一样	yīyàng	adj.	same, as…as…	17
鸭蛋	yādàn	n.	duck egg	18
要是	yàoshi	conj.	if, supposing	20
意外	yìwài	n. /adj.	accident; unexpected	21
英俊	yīngjùn	adj.	handsome	23
		Z		
这么	zhème	pron.	so, such	1
脏	zāng	adj.	dirty	1
主任	zhǔrèn	n.	director	1
志愿	zhìyuàn	n. /v.	aspiration; volunteer	2
尊敬	zūnjìng	v. /n.	to respect, to esteem; respect	2
总统	zǒngtǒng	n.	president	3
站	zhàn	v.	to stand	3
只	zhǐ/zhī	adv. /m.	only, solely; used for certain animals	4
座	zuò	m.	used for buildings, bridges, mountains, etc.	5
凿	záo	v.	to chisel	5
转	zhuǎn	v.	to turn, to shift	6
终于	zhōngyú	adv.	finally	6
最好	zuìhǎo	adv.	had better	6
最近	zuìjìn	adv.	lately, recently	7

续表 14

词语 Words/Phrases	拼音 Pinyin	词性 Parts of Speech	词义 Meanings	课号 Lesson
撞	zhuàng	v.	to bump against	7
照片	zhàopiàn	n.	photo	7
至于	zhìyú	prep.	as for, as to	7
长进	zhǎngjìn	v.	to make a progress, to improve	10
转移	zhuǎnyí	v.	to transfer, to shift	10
证明	zhèngmíng	v.	to prove	11
抓	zhuā	v.	to grab, to seize	12
装	zhuāng	v.	to pretend; to load	13
最后	zuìhòu	adj. /n.	last; the last one	13
仔	zǎi	n.	(of domestic animals) young	13
眨	zhǎ	v.	to blink, to wink	14
追	zhuī	v.	to chase, to go after	15
直接	zhíjiē	adj.	direct, straight	15
着火	zháo huǒ	v.	to catch fire	16
中	zhòng	v.	to win (in a lottery)	16
作弊	zuò bì	v.	to cheat	17
准	zhǔn	v. /adj.	to allow, to permit; exact, precise	17
自己	zìjǐ	pron.	self	18
种	zhǒng	m.	kind, type	18
总是	zǒngshì	adv.	always	18
嘴(巴)	zuǐ(ba)	n.	mouth	18
正好	zhènghǎo	adj. /adv.	just in time, just right	19
走运	zǒu yùn	v.	be in luck, be lucky	20
之后	zhīhòu	n.	after, hereafter	21
自从	zìcóng	prep.	ever since	23
睁	zhēng	v.	to open one's eyes	23